Distory

ALSO BY ROBERT SCHNAKENBERG

The Encyclopedia Shatnerica

ST. MARTIN'S PRESS

NEW YORK

Robert
Schnakenberg

Distory

A

TREASURY

OF

HISTORICAL

INSULTS

www.stmartins.com

ISBN 0-312-32671-8
EAN 978-0312-32671-5

First Edition: December 2004

10   9   8   7   6   5   4   3   2   1

CONTENTS

INTRODUCTION

*I*nsult has always played a part in human history. Wherever men and women have gathered in deliberative bodies, whenever great egos have clashed in the halls of power or on the battlefield, there historical figures have resorted to personal invective to cut their opponents and rivals down to size. This collection celebrates that heritage of calumny and the honesty of expression behind it.

While historical conflicts cannot simplistically be reduced to amplified personal quarrels, it's hard to ignore the way events of global import have a tendency to boil over in the form of petty rudeness. Political or territorial disputes often originate in self-interest and personal ambition, are expressed in terms of conflict, and occasionally find their terminus in outright paranoia. Remarks made off the cuff, particularly personal remarks, open a window on the true character of the speaker, revealing his or her innermost motivations. What did Napoleon *really* think of Wellington? Was the competition among Allied generals during World War II as intense as it seemed from the outside? We can learn a lot from what someone says in their least guarded moments.

Sadly, the golden age of insult may have passed. In recent years, there has been a discernible downshift in the level of rhetorical vituperation. The advent of gavel-to-gavel television coverage of deliberative proceedings, the desire on the part of the public for less partisan, less ideological politics, and the rise of political correctness have all conspired to muffle much of the rancor out of public discourse on both sides of the Atlantic. What has resulted is not more civil debate but merely less honest, less open debate. Even memoirs published many years after a person has receded from public life rarely contain the kind of pungent assessments of contemporaries contained in Merle Miller's delightfully profane oral biography of Harry Truman. They don't make insults, or politicians, like that anymore.

Some notes on the selection process are in order. With a

few exceptions, I have chosen to limit the scope of this book to insults uttered by world leaders, political and military figures, and well-known historical personages. The legendary one-liners of great wits and literary icons, from Dorothy Parker to T. S. Eliot, have been exhaustively compiled elsewhere and lay beyond the purview of this volume. This is a book about history and the men and women who made it.

For similar reasons, I have elected to include only a few quotations from professional journalists, historians, and political writers. The annals of newspaperdom are full of scathing editorials excoriating this or that historical figure in highly personal terms, particularly in the early American Republic; the book would quickly become elephantine with the weight of them. Besides, one expects a famously pithy observer like H. L. Mencken to have something memorable to say about the leading lights of his time. It's much more interesting, I think, to hear a great insult emerge from the lips of a more surprising source like, say, Warren G. Harding. As for historians, well, part of their job is to form considered opinions about historical events and figures based on evidence accrued over decades and centuries, not on ideology or personal antipathy. If they're resorting to insult, they probably aren't doing their job very well.

Finally, it is the destiny of a great quotation to be attributed to many different sources. I have made every effort to wade through the misattributions and weed out apocryphal quotes and sources. In some cases an insult was simply too good to leave out, despite a questionable parentage, and I have gone with the source I considered most reliable. My apologies to anyone, living or dead, whose wicked turn of phrase has not been credited properly.

DISUNITED STATES

FEUDIN' FOUNDERS

We have a tendency to look back at America's Founding Fathers as paragons of civil discourse. But the written record they left behind paints a decidedly less polite picture. Politics, it seems, has always been a contact sport. . . .

> This man has no principles, public or private. As a politician, his sole spring of action is an inordinate ambition.
>
> —ALEXANDER HAMILTON, ON AARON BURR

I never thought him an honest, frank-dealing man,
but considered him as a crooked gun . . . whose aim or
shot you could never be sure of.
—THOMAS JEFFERSON, ON AARON BURR

The bastard brat of a Scotch peddler.

A man devoid of every principle.

—JOHN ADAMS, ON ALEXANDER HAMILTON

A man without head and without heart—the mere
shadow of a man!
—JOHN ADAMS, ON JOHN HANCOCK

What a poor, ignorant, malicious, shortsighted,
crapulous mass, is Tom Paine's *Common Sense*.
—JOHN ADAMS, ON TOM PAINE

[That] mere adventurer from England, without fortune, without family or connections, ignorant even of grammar.

—GOUVERNEUR MORRIS, U.S. STATESMAN, ON TOM PAINE

[His] inveteracy is profound, and his mind of that gloomy malignity which will never let him forego the opportunity of satiating it on a victim.

—THOMAS JEFFERSON, ON JOHN MARSHALL, CHIEF JUSTICE OF THE SUPREME COURT

You and I were long friends; you are now my enemy, and I am

YOURS,

B. FRANKLIN,

—IN A LETTER TO WILLIAM STRAHAN, PRINTER AND PATRON OF THE ARTS

A crafty and lecherous old hypocrite whose very statue seems to gloat on the wenches as they walk the States House Yard.

—WILLIAM COBBETT, BRITISH RADICAL JOURNALIST, ON BENJAMIN FRANKLIN

Cobbett wasn't the only one to take swipes at the bespectacled, grandfatherly figure one recent biographer dubbed "the First American." Though beloved by many through the centuries, Franklin has had his share of detractors as well. . . .

A philosophical Quaker full of mean and thrifty maxims.
—JOHN KEATS, BRITISH POET

Benjamin Franklin, incarnation of the peddling, tuppenny Yankee.
—JEFFERSON DAVIS, CONFEDERATE PRESIDENT

He is our wise prophet of chicanery, the great buffoon.
—WILLIAM CARLOS WILLIAMS, U.S. POET

SPITE HOUSE

Never a people to stand on ceremony, Americans began insulting their presidents as soon as they started electing them. Some of the most baleful tidings came from fellow members of the White House fraternity—Teddy Roosevelt's

comments about Woodrow Wilson alone could probably fill
up an entire book (and quite an entertaining one at that).

One of the curious things one notes in looking over these
quotations is that some of America's most highly regarded
chief executives seem to have inspired the most bilious insults.
Perhaps a "shooting fish in a barrel" principle is at work
here. After all, anyone can take a potshot at, say, Warren
Harding, but it takes a refined animus to lob insults at a
Washington or a Lincoln. As this chief-by-chief rundown
suggests, there has been no shortage of volunteers in either
case. . . .

GEORGE WASHINGTON (1789–1797)

That Washington was not a scholar is certain. That
he is too illiterate, unlearned, unread for his station is
equally beyond dispute.
—JOHN ADAMS

That dark, designing, sordid, ambitious, vain, proud,
arrogant, and vindictive knave.
—GEN. CHARLES LEE, REVOLUTIONARY
COMMANDER

5

If ever a nation was debauched by a man, the American nation has been debauched by Washington. . . . If ever a nation was deceived by a man, the American nation has been deceived by Washington.

—Benjamin Franklin Bache,
U.S. journalist and grandson of
Benjamin Franklin

[A]nd as to you, sir, treacherous in private friendship . . . and a hypocrite in public life, the world will be puzzled to decide whether you are an apostate or an imposter, whether you have abandoned good principles, or whether you ever had?

—Tom Paine

Insane.

—James Monroe

JOHN ADAMS (1797–1801)

It has been the political career of this man to begin with hypocrisy, proceed with arrogance, and finish with contempt.

—Tom Paine

He is distrustful, obstinate, excessively vain, and takes no counsel from anyone . . . He is vain, irritable, and a bad calculator of the force and probable effect of the motives which govern men.

    —THOMAS JEFFERSON

Always an honest man, often a great one, but sometimes absolutely mad.

    —BENJAMIN FRANKLIN

You have no idea of the meanness, indecency, almost insanity of his conduct.

    —ALBERT GALLATIN, U.S. TREASURY
       SECRETARY, IN A LETTER TO HIS WIFE

A ruffian deserving of the curses of mankind.

    —BENJAMIN FRANKLIN BACHE,
       U.S. JOURNALIST AND GRANDSON OF
       BENJAMIN FRANKLIN

I should be deficient in candor were I to conceal the conviction, that he does not possess the talents adapted to the administration of government, and that there are great and intrinsic defects in his character which unfit him for the office of Chief Magistrate.

Petty, mean, egotistic, erratic, eccentric, jealous natured, and hot tempered.

—ALEXANDER HAMILTON

The reign of Mr. Adams has, hitherto, been one continued tempest of malignant passions. As president, he has never opened his lips, or lifted his pen, without threatening and scolding. The grand object of his administration has been to exasperate the rage of contending parties, to calumniate and destroy every man who differs from his opinions.

—JAMES CALLENDER, U.S. JOURNALIST

Whether he is spiteful, playful, witty, kind, cold, drunk, sober, angry, easy, stiff, jealous, cautious, close, open, it is always in the wrong place or to the wrong person.

—JAMES MCHENRY, SECRETARY OF WAR IN
ADAMS'S ADMINISTRATION

God forgive me for the vile thought, but I cannot help thinking of a monkey just put into breeches when I see him betray such evident marks of self-conceit.

—WILLIAM MACLAY, U.S. SENATOR

It's just that he wasn't very special.

—HARRY S TRUMAN

THOMAS JEFFERSON (1801–1809)

The moral character of Jefferson was repulsive. Continually puling about liberty, equality, and the degrading curse of slavery, he brought his own children to the hammer, and money of his debaucheries.

—ALEXANDER HAMILTON

Instead of being the ardent pursuer of science some think him, he is indolent and his soul is poisoned with ambition.

It is with much reluctance that I am obliged to look upon him as a man whose mind is warped by prejudice and so blinded by ignorance as to be unfit for the office he holds. However wise and scientific as philosopher, as a politician he is a child and a dupe of the party.

—John Adams

A slur upon the moral government of the world.
   —John Quincy Adams

Perhaps the most incapable executive that ever filled the presidential chair . . . it would be difficult to imagine a man less fit to guide the state with honor and safety through the stormy times that marked the opening of the present century.
   —Theodore Roosevelt

JAMES MADISON (1809–1817)

A withered little applejohn.
—WASHINGTON IRVING

I do not like his looks any better than I like his administration.
—DANIEL WEBSTER

JAMES MONROE (1817–1825)

One of the most improper and incompetent that could be selected [for president]. Naturally dull and stupid; extremely illiterate; indecisive to a degree that would be incredible to one who did not know him . . . he has no opinion on any subject and will always be under the government of the worst men.
—AARON BURR

[H]is talents were exercised not in grandeur but in mediocrity.
—ARTHUR STYRON, U.S. AUTHOR

A mere tool in the hands of the French government.
—GEORGE WASHINGTON

> A pretty minor president. In spite of the Monroe Doctrine. That's the only important thing he ever did more or less on his own, when you really get down to it.
> —HARRY S TRUMAN

JOHN QUINCY ADAMS (1825–1829)

His disposition is as perverse and mulish as that of his father.
—JAMES BUCHANAN

It is said he is a disgusting man to do business. Coarse, dirty, clownish in his address, and stiff and abstracted in his opinions, which are drawn from books exclusively.
—WILLIAM HENRY HARRISON

Of all the men whom it was ever my lot to accost and to waste civilities upon, [he] was the most doggedly and systematically repulsive.
—W. H. LYTTLETON, GOVERNOR OF
NORTH CAROLINA

I just don't think there were any events in Adams's
administration that were very interesting.
   —HARRY S TRUMAN

ANDREW JACKSON (1829–1837)

I feel much alarmed at the prospect of seeing General
Jackson president. He is the most unfit man I know
for such a place . . . he is a dangerous man.
   —THOMAS JEFFERSON

He is ignorant, passionate, hypocritical, corrupt, and
easily swayed by the basest men who surround him.

I cannot believe that the killing of two thousand
Englishmen at New Orleans qualifies a person for the
various difficult and complicated duties of the
presidency.

Except [for] an enormous fabric of executive power
for himself, the president has built up nothing,
constructed nothing, and will leave no enduring

"monument of his administration. He goes for destruction, universal destruction; and it seems to be his greatest ambition to efface and obliterate every trace of the wisdom of his predecessors.

—HENRY CLAY

A barbarian who cannot write a sentence of grammar and can hardly spell his own name.

Incompetent both by his ignorance and by the fury of his passions.

—JOHN QUINCY ADAMS

Little advanced in civilization over the Indians with whom he made war.

—ELIJAH HUNT MILLS, U.S. SENATOR

MARTIN VAN BUREN (1837–1841)

His principles are all subordinate to his ambitions.
—JOHN QUINCY ADAMS

Mr. Van Buren became offended with me at the
beginning of my administration because I chose to
exercise my own judgment in the selection of my own
cabinet, and would not be controlled by him and
suffer him to select it for me. Mr. Van Buren is the
most fallen man I have ever known.
—JAMES K. POLK

Van Buren is as opposite to General Jackson as dung
is to diamond. . . . He is what the English call a
dandy. When he enters the Senate chamber in the
morning, he struts and swaggers like a crow in the
gutter. He is laced up in corsets, such as women in
town wear, and, if possible, tighter than the best of
them. It would be difficult to say, from his personal
appearance, whether he was man or woman, but for
his large red and gray whiskers.
—DAVY CROCKETT

He is not . . . of the race of the lion or the tiger; he belongs to a lower order: the fox.
—JOHN C. CALHOUN

He rowed to his object with muffled oars.
—JOHN RANDOLPH, U.S. SENATOR

He was just a politician and nothing more, a politician who was out of his depth.
—HARRY S TRUMAN

WILLIAM HENRY HARRISON (1841)

He is as tickled with the presidency as is a young woman with a new bonnet.
—MARTIN VAN BUREN

Our Present Imbecile Chief.
—ANDREW JACKSON

[An] active but shallow mind, a political adventurer not without talents but self-sufficient, vain, and indiscreet.

The greatest beggar and the most troublesome of all the office seekers during my administration was General Harrison.

—John Quincy Adams

Some folks are silly enough to have formed a plan to make a president of the U.S. out of this clerk and clodhopper.
—William Henry Harrison, on himself

Harrison didn't accomplish a thing during the month he was in office. He made no contribution whatsoever. He had no policy. He didn't know what the government was about, to tell the truth. About the only thing he did during that brief period was see friends and friends of friends, because he was such an easy mark that he couldn't say no to anybody, and everybody and his brother was beseeching him for jobs.
—Harry S Truman

JOHN TYLER (1841–1845)

A slave-monger whose talents are not above mediocrity, and with a spirit incapable of expansion to the dimensions of the station upon which he has been cast by the hand of providence.
    —JOHN QUINCY ADAMS

A politician of monumental littleness.
    —THEODORE ROOSEVELT

He was a contrary old son of a bitch.
    —HARRY S TRUMAN

JAMES K. POLK (1845–1849)

May God save the country, for it is evident that the people will not.
    —MILLARD FILLMORE, ON POLK'S ELECTION TO
    THE PRESIDENCY

I never betrayed a friend or was guilty of the black sin of ingratitude. Mr. Polk cannot say as much.
    —ANDREW JACKSON

A victim of the use of water as a beverage.
    —Sam Houston

Polk . . . is just qualified for an eminent County Court
lawyer. . . . He has no wit, no literature, no point of
argument, no gracefulness of delivery, no eloquence
of language, no philosophy, no pathos, no felicitous
impromptus; nothing that can constitute an orator,
but confidence, fluency, and labor.
    —John Quincy Adams

A bewildered, confounded, and miserably perplexed man.
    —Abraham Lincoln

He has a set of interested parasites about him, who
flatter him until he does not know himself. He seems
to be acting upon the principle of hanging an old
friend for the purpose of making two new ones.
    —Andrew Johnson

ZACHARY TAYLOR (1849–1850)

General Taylor is, I have no doubt, a well-meaning
old man. He is, however, uneducated, exceedingly

ignorant of public affairs, and I should judge, of very ordinary capacity.

 —JAMES K. POLK

Quite ignorant for his rank, and quite bigoted in his ignorance.

 —WINFIELD SCOTT, U.S. GENERAL AND
  POLITICIAN

Old Zack is a good old soul, but don't know himself from a side of sole leather in the way of statesmanship.

 —HORACE GREELEY

A most simple-minded old man. . . . It is remarkable that such a man should be president of the United States.

 —HORACE MANN, U.S. EDUCATOR

One of the do-nothing presidents.

 —HARRY S TRUMAN

MILLARD FILLMORE (1850–1853)

A vain and handsome mediocrity.
  —GLYNDON G. VAN DEUSEN,
    U.S. BIOGRAPHER

He was a man who changed with the wind, and as president of the United States he didn't do anything that's worth pointing out.
  —HARRY S TRUMAN

FRANKLIN PIERCE (1853–1857)

A small politician, of low capacity and mean surroundings, proud to act as the servile tool of men worse than himself but also stronger and abler.
  —THEODORE ROOSEVELT

Whoever may be elected, we cannot get a poorer cuss than now disgraces the presidential chair!
  —BENJAMIN BROWN FRENCH, CLERK OF THE
    U.S. HOUSE OF REPRESENTATIVES

> A complete fizzle. . . . Pierce didn't know what was going on, and even if he had, he wouldn't have known what to do about it.
> —HARRY S TRUMAN

JAMES BUCHANAN (1857–1861)

> There is no such person running as James Buchanan. He is dead of lockjaw. Nothing remains but a platform and a bloated mass of political putridity.
> —THADDEUS STEVENS, U.S. CONGRESSMAN

> The Constitution provides for every accidental contingency in the executive—except a vacancy in the mind of the president.
> —JOHN SHERMAN, U.S. SENATOR

> All his acts and opinions seem to be with a view to his own advancement. . . . Mr. Buchanan is an able man, but is in small matters without judgment and sometimes acts like an old maid.
> —JAMES K. POLK

> Buchanan . . . hesitated and backtracked and felt that his constitutional prerogative didn't allow him to do

things, and he ended up doing absolutely nothing and threw everything into Lincoln's lap.

—Harry S Truman

ABRAHAM LINCOLN (1861–1865)

He is a huckster in politics; a first-rate second-rate man.

—Wendell Phillips, U.S. abolitionist

His mind works in the right directions but seldom works clearly and cleanly. His bread is of unbolted flour, and much straw, too, mixes in the bran, and sometimes gravel stones.

—Henry Ward Beecher, U.S. abolitionist
    and clergyman

Filthy storyteller, despot, liar, thief, braggart, buffoon, usurper, monster, ignoramus Abe, old scoundrel, perjurer, swindler, tyrant, field-butcher, land-pirate.

—*Harpers* magazine

Nothing more than a well-meaning baboon.

An offensive exhibition of boorishness and vulgarity.

I went to the White House shortly after tea where I found 'the original gorilla,' about as intelligent as ever. What a specimen to be at the head of our affairs now!

—Gen. George McClellan

To the extent of his limited ability and narrow intelligence the willing instrument [of the abolitionists] for all the woe which [has] thus far been brought upon the country and for all the degradation, all the atrocity, all the desolation and ruin.
   —Franklin Pierce

This man's appearance, his pedigree, his coarse low jokes and anecdotes, his vulgar similes and his frivolity, are a disgrace to the seat he holds.
   —John Wilkes Booth

ANDREW JOHNSON (1865–1869)

He is very vindictive and perverse in his temper and conduct.

—JAMES K. POLK

Every Rebel guerrilla and jayhawker, every man who ran to Canada to avoid the draft, every bounty hunter, every deserter, every cowardly sneak that ran from danger and disgraced his flag, every man who loves slavery and hates liberty . . . and every villain, of whatever name or crime, who loves power more than justice, slavery more than freedom, is a Democrat and an endorser of Andrew Johnson.

—JAMES A. GARFIELD

I have never been so tired of anything before as I have been with the political speeches of Mr. Johnson . . . I look upon them as a national disgrace.

He is such an infernal liar.

—ULYSSES S. GRANT

> [He] reduced the presidency to the level of a grog
> house.
>   —JOHN SHERMAN, U.S. SENATOR

He is surrounded, hampered, tangled in the meshes of
his own wickedness. Unfortunate, unhappy man,
behold your doom!

You will remember that in Egypt He sent frogs, locusts,
murrain, lice, and finally demanded the firstborn of
every one of the oppressors. We have been oppressed
with taxes and debts, and He has sent us worse than
lice, and has afflicted us with Andrew Johnson.

—THADDEUS STEVENS, U.S. CONGRESSMAN

ULYSSES S. GRANT (1869–1877)

He has done more than any other president to
degrade the character of cabinet officers by choosing

them in the model of the military staff, because of their personal relation to him and not because of their national reputation and the public needs. . . . His imperturbability is amazing. I am in doubt whether to call it greatness or stupidity.

—JAMES GARFIELD

He is a scientific Goth, resembling Alaric, destroying the country as he goes and delivering the people over to starvation. Nor does he bury his dead, but leaves them to rot on the battlefield.

—JOHN TYLER

He decidedly prefers the delights of a horserace to the tedious work of a cabinet meeting. . . . It is the closest approach to the habits of royal courts this country has ever witnessed.

—CARL SCHURZ, U.S. SENATOR

Early in 1869 the cry was for 'no politicians,' but the country did not mean 'no brains.'

—WILLIAM CLAFLIN, GOVERNOR OF MASSACHUSETTS

The people are tired of a man who has not an idea above a horse or a cigar.
   —Joseph Brown, governor of Georgia

A study of the presidency from Washington to Grant is sufficient to disprove Darwin.
   —Henry Adams, U.S. historian and
   presidential grandson

He combined great gifts with great mediocrity.
   —Woodrow Wilson

The worst president in our history.
   —Harry S Truman

RUTHERFORD B. HAYES (1877–1881)

This administration will be the greatest failure the country has ever saw.
   —Samuel Tilden, governor of New York
   (defeated by Hayes in the controversial
   election of 1876)

A third-rate nonentity, whose only recommendation
is that he is obnoxious to no one.

—HENRY ADAMS, U.S. HISTORIAN AND
   PRESIDENTIAL GRANDSON

The [Southern] policy of the president has turned out
to be a giveaway from the beginning. He has nolled
suits, discontinued prosecutions, offered conciliation
everywhere in the South while they have spent their
time in whetting their knives for any Republican they
could find.

—JAMES GARFIELD

Mr. Hayes came in by a majority of one, and goes out
by unanimous consent.

—ANONYMOUS HAYES ADVISER

He had no real hold upon the country. His amiable
character, his lack of party heat, his conciliatory
attitude towards the South alienated rather than
attracted the members of his party in Congress. . . .
The Democrats did not like him because he seemed
to them incapable of frank, consistent action.

—WOODROW WILSON

Elected by a fluke and knew it.
   —HARRY S TRUMAN

JAMES A. GARFIELD (1881)

Garfield has shown that he is not possessed of the
backbone of an angleworm.
   —ULYSSES S. GRANT

He rushes into a fight with the horns of a bull and the
skin of a rabbit.
   —JEREMIAH BLACK, U.S. SECRETARY OF STATE

He was not executive in his talents—not original, not
firm, not a moral force. He leaned on others—could
not face a frowning world; his habits suffered from
Washington life. His course at various times when
trouble came betrayed weakness.
   —RUTHERFORD B. HAYES

CHESTER A. ARTHUR (1881–1885)

A nonentity with side-whiskers.
   —WOODROW WILSON

Nothing like it ever before in the Executive
Mansion—liquor, snobbery, and worse.

    —RUTHERFORD B. HAYES

The only thing that stands out about Arthur is that
he took all the wonderful furniture that had been
brought to this country by Jefferson, Monroe, and
several of the other presidents of that period and sold
it in an auction for about $6,500.

    —HARRY S TRUMAN

GROVER CLEVELAND (1885–1889, 1893–1897)

He sailed through American history like a steel ship
loaded with monoliths of granite.

    —H. L. MENCKEN

To nominate Grover Cleveland would be to march
through a slaughterhouse into an open grave.

    —HENRY WATTERSON, U.S. JOURNALIST

> We have been told that the mantle of Tilden has fallen upon Cleveland. The mantle of a giant upon the shoulders of a dwarf.
>
> —WILLIAM BOURKE COCKRAN,
> U.S. CONGRESSMAN

What in the world had Grover Cleveland done? Will you tell me? You give up? I have been looking for six weeks for a Democrat who could tell me what Cleveland has done for the good of his country and for the benefit of the people, but I have not found him. . . . He says himself . . . that two-thirds of his time has been uselessly spent with Democrats who want office. . . . Now he has been so occupied in that way that he has not done anything else.

—WILLIAM McKINLEY

BENJAMIN HARRISON (1889–1893)

Damn the president! He is a cold-blooded, narrow-minded, prejudiced, obstinate, timid old psalm-singing Indianapolis politician.

—THEODORE ROOSEVELT

As glacial as a Siberian stripped of his fur.
  —Tom Platt, U.S. senator

There's not much else you can say about Harrison
except that he was president of the United States.
  —Harry S Truman

WILLIAM MCKINLEY (1897–1901)

I was more struck than ever with his mask. It is a
genuine Italian ecclesiastical face of the fifteenth
century. And there are idiots who think Mark Hanna
will run him!
  —John Hay, McKinley's future secretary
    of state, after a visit to then-
    Governor McKinley's Ohio home

McKinley has a chocolate éclair backbone.
  —Theodore Roosevelt

Why, if a man were to call my dog McKinley, and the
brute failed to resent to the death the . . . insult, I'd
drown it.
  —William Cowper Brann, U.S. journalist

He walked among men a bronze statue, for thirty
years determinedly looking for his pedestal.
  —WILLIAM ALLEN WHITE, U.S. JOURNALIST

McKinley keeps his ear to the ground so close that he
gets it full of grasshoppers much of the time.
  —JOSEPH CANNON, U.S. CONGRESSMAN

McKinley didn't turn out to be much of a president.
  —HARRY S TRUMAN

THEODORE ROOSEVELT (1901–1909)

Now look, that damned cowboy is president of the
United States!
  —MARK HANNA, U.S. SENATOR

He is the most dangerous man of the age.

What's the use of wasting good serviceable
indignation on him?
  —WOODROW WILSON

One of the most fantastic and impudent political liars in America . . . as selfish as a sponge!

—GEORGE WASHINGTON COOK,
U.S. CONGRESSMAN

Well, the mad Roosevelt has a new achievement to his credit. He succeeded in defeating the party that furnished him a job for nearly all of his manhood days after leaving the ranch. . . . The eminent fakir can now turn to raising hell, his specialty, along other lines.

—WARREN HARDING

Mr. Roosevelt likens himself to Abraham Lincoln more and resembles him less than any man in the history of this country. . . . I hold that the man is a demagogue and a flatterer who comes out and tells the people that they know it all. I hate a flatterer. I like a man to tell the truth straight out, and I hate to see a man try to honeyfugle the people.

> A megalomaniac.
>
> —WILLIAM HOWARD TAFT

Theodore Roosevelt was always getting himself in hot water by talking before he had to commit himself upon issues not well defined.

—CALVIN COOLIDGE

He had his troubles with Congress and he had his troubles with the trusts, and he didn't get a heck of a lot done. . . . He ended up adding up to more talk than achievement.

—HARRY S TRUMAN

WILLIAM HOWARD TAFT (1909–1913)

It's very difficult for me to understand how a man who is so good as Chief Justice could have been so bad as president.

—LOUIS BRANDEIS, SUPREME COURT JUSTICE

A flubdub with a streak of the second rate and the common in him. . . . [A] fathead and a puzzlewit.

Taft meant well, but he meant well feebly.

—THEODORE ROOSEVELT

A fat, jolly, likeable, mediocre man.
   —HARRY S TRUMAN

WOODROW WILSON (1913–1921)

The air currents of the world never ventilated his mind.
   —WALTER HINES PAGE, U.S. JOURNALIST

He is a silly doctrinaire at times and an utterly selfish and cold-blooded politician always.

A damned Presbyterian hypocrite, and a Byzantine logothete.

An infernal skunk in the White House.

—THEODORE ROOSEVELT

How can I talk to a fellow who thinks himself the first man in two thousand years to know anything about peace on earth?
    —GEORGES CLEMENCEAU, FRENCH PRIME
        MINISTER

I regard him as a ruthless hypocrite and as an opportunist, who has not convictions he would not barter at once for votes.

I feel certain that he would not recognize a generous impulse if he met it on the street.

—WILLIAM HOWARD TAFT

The spacious philanthropy which he exhaled upon Europe stopped quite sharply at the coasts of his own country.

—WINSTON CHURCHILL

WARREN G. HARDING (1921–1923)

Harding was not a bad man. He was just a slob.

—ALICE ROOSEVELT LONGWORTH, DAUGHTER OF THEODORE ROOSEVELT

His speeches left the impression of an army of pompous phrases moving over the landscape in search of an idea.

—WILLIAM McADOO, FORMER SECRETARY OF THE TREASURY

A tinhorn politician with the manner of a rural corn doctor and the mien of a ham actor.

He writes the worst English that I have ever encountered. It reminds me of a string of wet sponges;

it reminds me of tattered washing on the line; it reminds me of stale bean soup, of dogs barking through endless nights. It is so bad that a sort of grandeur creeps into it. It drags itself out of the dark abyss of pish and crawls insanely up the topmost pinnacle of posh. It is flap and doodle. It is balder and dash.

—H. L. Mencken

The only man, woman, or child who ever wrote a simple declarative sentence with seven grammatical errors.

—E. E. Cummings

He has a bungalow mind.

Harding is incapable of thought, because he has nothing to think with.

—Woodrow Wilson

He was not a man with either the experience or the intellectual quality that the position needed.

—HERBERT HOOVER

I am not fit for this office and never should have been here.

—WARREN G. HARDING, ON HIMSELF

CALVIN COOLIDGE (1923–1929)

He looks as if he had been weaned on a pickle.

—ALICE ROOSEVELT LONGWORTH, DAUGHTER
OF THEODORE ROOSEVELT

How could they tell?

—DOROTHY PARKER, U.S. WRITER, ON BEING
TOLD THAT COOLIDGE HAD DIED

Calvin Coolidge didn't say much, and when he did, he didn't say much.

—WILL ROGERS

Calvin Coolidge's perpetual expression was of smelling something burning on the stove.
—SHERWIN L. COOK, U.S. CONGRESSMAN

He slept more than any other president, whether by day or by night. Nero fiddled, but Coolidge only snored.
—H. L. MENCKEN

An economic fatalist with a God-given inertia. He knew nothing and refused to learn.

This runty, aloof little man who quacks through his nose when he speaks.

—WILLIAM ALLEN WHITE, U.S. JOURNALIST

Distinguishable from the furniture only when he moved.
—GEORGE CREEL, WILSON ADMINISTRATION OFFICIAL

I always figured the American public wanted a
solemn ass for president, so I went along with them.
  —CALVIN COOLIDGE

HERBERT HOOVER (1929–1933)

Hoover, if elected, will do one thing that is almost
incomprehensible to the human mind: he will make a
great man out of Coolidge.
  —CLARENCE DARROW

He wouldn't commit himself to the time of day from
a hat full of watches.
  —WESTBROOK PEGLER, U.S. JOURNALIST

I have the feeling that he would rather see a good
cause fail than succeed if he were not the head of it.
  —WOODROW WILSON

Such a little man could not have made so big a
depression.
  —NORMAN THOMAS, U.S. SOCIALIST
    POLITICIAN

If you put a rose in Hoover's hand it would melt.
—GUTZON BORGLUM, MOUNT RUSHMORE
SCULPTOR

That man has offered me unsolicited advice for six
years, all of it bad.
—CALVIN COOLIDGE

A private meeting with Hoover is like sitting in a
bath of ink.
—HENRY STIMSON, U.S. SECRETARY OF WAR

Facts to Hoover's brain are as water to a sponge; they
are absorbed into every tiny interstice.
—BERNARD M. BARUCH, U.S. FINANCIER

FRANKLIN D. ROOSEVELT (1933–1945)

A chameleon on plaid.
—HERBERT HOOVER

Two-thirds mush and one-third Eleanor.
—ALICE ROOSEVELT LONGWORTH, DAUGHTER
OF THEODORE ROOSEVELT

The man who started more creations since Genesis—
and finished none.

— Hugh Johnson, U.S. New Deal
  administrator

If he became convinced tomorrow that coming out
for cannibalism would get him the votes he sorely
needs, he would begin fattening a missionary in the
White House backyard come Wednesday.

— H. L. Mencken

Thousands of pictures were taken, and none for the
glory of the troops; all for the glory of FDR.

— Gen. George S. Patton

HARRY S TRUMAN (1945–1953)

Harry Truman proves that old adage that any man
can become president of the United States.

— Norman Thomas, U.S. Socialist
  politician

Miss Truman cannot sing very well. She is flat a good
deal of the time . . . she communicates almost
nothing of the music she presents. . . . There are few

moments during her recital when one can relax and feel confident that she will make her goal, which is the end of the song.
—PAUL HUME, WASHINGTON POST MUSIC
    CRITIC, REVIEWING A RECITAL BY MARGARET
    TRUMAN, THE PRESIDENT'S DAUGHTER

I have just read your lousy review buried in the back pages. You sound like a frustrated old man who never made a success, an eight-ulcer man on a four-ulcer job, and all four ulcers working. I have never met you, but if I do you'll need a new nose and plenty of beefsteak and perhaps a supporter below.
—HARRY S TRUMAN, IN HIS LETTER OF REPLY
    TO HUME

It defies all common sense to send that roughneck ward politician back to the White House.
—ROBERT TAFT, U.S. SENATOR

DWIGHT D. EISENHOWER (1953–1961)

A cardiac case whose chief interest is in getting away from his job as often as possible for golf and bridge.
—I. F. STONE, U.S. JOURNALIST

He's just a coward. He hasn't got any backbone at all.

Why, this fellow don't know any more about politics than a pig knows about Sunday.

—Harry S Truman

If I talk over the people's head, Ike must be talking under their feet.

The General has dedicated himself so many times, he must feel like the cornerstone of a public building.

—Adlai Stevenson

I don't know how many times I pulled that bumbling, brainlack bubblehead's chestnuts out of the fire and he never thanked me once.
    —Lyndon Johnson

JOHN F. KENNEDY (1961–1963)

> How can a guy this politically immature seriously expect to be president?
> —FRANKLIN D. ROOSEVELT JR.

I sincerely fear for my country if Jack Kennedy should be elected president. The fellow has absolutely no principles. Money and gall are all the Kennedys have.

   —BARRY GOLDWATER

The first time I met Jack Kennedy, I couldn't believe this skinny pasty-looking kid was a candidate for anything.

   —THOMAS P. "TIP" O'NEILL,
   U.S. CONGRESSMAN

His difficulty appears to stem primarily from an inadequate understanding of our American system—of how it really works, of the psychological, motivational, and economic factors that make it ebb and flow.

   —DWIGHT D. EISENHOWER

Kennedy concentrated on building up what I characterized as a 'poor mouth' image of America. . . . He seized on every possible shortcoming and inequity in American life, and promised immediate cure-alls.

—RICHARD NIXON

The enviably attractive nephew who sings an Irish ballad for the company and then winsomely disappears before the table clearing and dishwashing begin.

—LYNDON B. JOHNSON

LYNDON B. JOHNSON (1963–1969)

He is a small man. He doesn't have the depth of mind nor the breadth of vision to carry great responsibility. . . . Johnson is superficial and opportunistic.

—DWIGHT D. EISENHOWER

He exuded a brutal lust for power which I found most disagreeable. . . . He was a monster.

—DENIS HEALEY, BRITISH LABOUR POLITICIAN

He turned out to be so many different characters he could have populated all of *War and Peace* and still had a few people left over.

—HERBERT MITGANG, U.S. JOURNALIST

His skin is a millionth of an inch thick.

He fiddled while Detroit burned and he faddled while men died in Vietnam.

—BARRY GOLDWATER, U.S. SENATOR

Henry Clay always said he'd rather be right than president. Now President Johnson has proved it really is a choice.

—GERALD FORD

Why don't people like me?
Because, Mr. President, you're not a very likable man.

—EXCHANGE BETWEEN LYNDON JOHNSON AND SECRETARY OF STATE DEAN ACHESON

RICHARD M. NIXON (1969–1974)

He was a foul caricature of himself, a man with no soul, no inner convictions, with the integrity of a hyena and the style of a poison toad.
   —HUNTER S. THOMPSON, U.S. JOURNALIST

Richard Nixon is a no-good lying bastard. He can lie out of both sides of his mouth at the same time, and if he ever caught himself telling the truth, he'd lie just to keep his hand in.
   —HARRY S TRUMAN

Nixon is the kind of politician who would cut down a redwood tree and then mount the stump to make a speech for conservation.

McCarthyism in a white collar.

I recoil at the prospect of Mr. Nixon as custodian of this nation's future.

   —ADLAI STEVENSON

"

He's a cheap bastard; that's all there is to it.

He is a filthy, lying son of a bitch, and a very dangerous man.

—John F. Kennedy

I may not know much, but I know chicken shit from chicken salad. . . . He's like a Spanish horse, who runs faster than anyone for the first nine lengths, and then turns around and runs backwards. You'll see; he'll do something wrong in the end. He always does.
    —Lyndon Johnson

Avoid all needle drugs—the only dope worth shooting is Richard Nixon.
    —Abbie Hoffman, U.S. political activist

He is congenitally devious. When you talk to Nixon, you have no idea if his words actually reflect what's in his mind. It's something like kissing a girl through a handkerchief.

—EMMANUEL CELLAR, U.S. CONGRESSMAN

He bleeds people. He draws every drop of blood and then drops them from a cliff. He'll blame any person he can put his foot on.

—MARTHA MITCHELL, WIFE OF NIXON'S ATTORNEY GENERAL JOHN MITCHELL

GERALD R. FORD (1974–1977)

He's consistently wrong, and consistency is a virtue of small minds. He's never proposed a constructive solution to anything.

—ROBERT F. DRINAN, U.S. CONGRESSMAN

Jerry Ford is so dumb that he can't fart and chew gum at the same time.

He's a nice guy, but he played too much football with his helmet off.

—LYNDON B. JOHNSON

Richard Nixon impeached himself. He gave us Gerald Ford as his revenge.

—BELLA ABZUG, U.S. CONGRESSWOMAN

JIMMY CARTER (1977–1981)

He is your typical smiling, brilliant, back-stabbing, bull-shitting Southern nut-cutter.

—LANE KIRKLAND, U.S. LABOR LEADER

He's cold, cunning, cruel, and will destroy anything or anyone who stands in his way. . . . He's a typical politician, the type of person I have always detested in campaigning or in public office.

—LESTER MADDOX, GOVERNOR OF GEORGIA

They say Carter is the first businessman ever to sit in the White House. But why did they have to send us a small businessman?

—GEORGE MEANY, U.S. LABOR LEADER

Carter was so inexperienced that no one could make up such lack of information unless he was a genius, which he hadn't demonstrated. Then, when he said he was going to take up speed reading, I knew the cause was lost.

—EUGENE MCCARTHY, U.S. SENATOR

Jimmy Carter wants to speak loudly and carry a fly swatter.

—GERALD FORD

I once called Carter a 'chicken-fried McGovern,' and I take that back because I've come to respect McGovern.

—BOB DOLE, U.S. SENATOR

A complete birdbrain.

—JOHN LE BOUTILLIER, U.S. CONGRESSMAN

RONALD REAGAN (1981–1989)

He doesn't dye his hair—he's just prematurely orange.
—GERALD FORD

We've got the kind of president who thinks that arms control means some kind of deodorant.
—PAT SCHROEDER, U.S. CONGRESSWOMAN

He has done for monetarism what the Boston Strangler did for door-to-door salesmen.
—DENIS HEALEY, BRITISH LABOUR POLITICIAN

A triumph of the embalmer's art.
—GORE VIDAL

The pruneface from the West.
—COLEMAN YOUNG, MAYOR OF DETROIT

A cruel man with a steady smile.
—RALPH NADER

I don't like to attack Ronald Reagan as being too old for the job, but I remember that in his first movie Gabby Hayes got the girl.
—WALTER MONDALE

He can't decide whether he was born in a log cabin or a manger.

— BARRY GOLDWATER

He doesn't work very hard; he doesn't immerse himself in issues . . . he doesn't spend a lot of time thinking about things. . . . What bothers me most is that he seems not to be educable.

— ANTHONY BEILENSON, U.S. CONGRESSMAN

The youthful sparkle in his eyes is caused by his contact lenses, which he keeps highly polished.

— SHEILA GRAHAM, U.S. GOSSIP COLUMNIST

GEORGE BUSH (1989–1993)

He was born with a silver foot in his mouth.

— ANN RICHARDS, GOVERNOR OF TEXAS

The Joe Isuzu of American politics.

— MICHAEL DUKAKIS, GOVERNOR OF MASSACHUSETTS

If ignorance ever goes to forty dollars a barrel, I want drilling rights on George Bush's head.
—JIM HIGHTOWER, TEXAS AGRICULTURE COMMISSIONER

He would not know a principle if it were stuck on the end of an Exocet and smashed straight through his head.
—TONY BANKS, BRITISH LABOUR POLITICIAN

He's a Boy Scout with a hormone imbalance.
—KEVIN PHILLIPS, REPUBLICAN STRATEGIST

A pin-stripin' polo-playin' umbrella-totin' Ivy-leaguer, born with a silver spoon so far in his mouth that you couldn't get it out with a crowbar.
—BILL BAXLEY, ALABAMA ATTORNEY GENERAL

He's never had to do a day's work in his life.
—BOB DOLE

Bill Clinton's foreign policy experience is pretty much confined to having had breakfast once at the International House of Pancakes.

  —PAT BUCHANAN

The prince of sleaze.

  —JERRY BROWN

When I was president, I said I was a Ford, not a Lincoln. Well what we have now is a convertible Dodge.

  —GERALD FORD

It is the first time Clinton has ever rejected pussy in his life.

  —G. GORDON LIDDY, ON REPORTS THAT
    CLINTON WAS GIVING AWAY HIS PET CAT,
    SOCKS

He's not a statesman. He just acts for short-term gain.

  —JEAN CHRÉTIEN, CANADIAN PRIME MINISTER

Say what you want about the president, but we know his friends have convictions.

If I were in the president's place I would not have gotten a chance to resign. I would be laying in a pool of my own blood, hearing Mrs. Armey standing over me saying, 'How do I reload this damn thing?'
  —DICK ARMEY, U.S. CONGRESSMAN

I'm just sick and tired of presidents who jog. Remember, if Bill Clinton wins, we're going to have another four years of his white thighs flapping in the wind.
  —ARIANNA HUFFINGTON, U.S. NEWSPAPER
  COLUMNIST

Last time I saw [Clinton] he was swinging on the chandelier in the Oval Office with a brassiere around his head, Viagra in one hand and a Bible in the other, and he was torn between good and evil.
  —JAMES TRAFICANT, U.S. CONGRESSMAN

The president looked me in the eye and told me the same thing on several occasions. And I'm not upset. You want to know why? Because I never believed him in the first place.

 —ROBERT TORRICELLI, U.S. SENATOR

Nobody likes to be called a liar, but to be called a liar by Bill Clinton is really a unique experience.

 —H. ROSS PEROT

GEORGE W. BUSH (2001–)

Unusually incurious, abnormally unintelligent, amazingly inarticulate, fantastically uncultured, extraordinarily uneducated, and apparently quite proud of all these things.

 —CHRISTOPHER HITCHENS, BRITISH
  JOURNALIST

Logically unsound, confused and unprincipled, unwise to the extreme.

 —JIANG ZEMIN, CHINESE PRESIDENT

> Hopefully, he is not as stupid as he seems, nor as
> Mafia-like as his predecessors were.
>
> Bush was not elected president, but appointed, and
> therefore why should the U.S. bitch about Cuba not
> holding free elections?

—Fidel Castro

I have been disappointed in almost everything he has
done.
—Jimmy Carter

A shallow, arrogant, gun-loving, abortion-hating,
Christian fundamentalist Texan buffoon.
—unnamed European official, quoted in
the *New York Times*

The world expects something more of an American
president than to prance around on a flight deck
dressed up like a pilot.
—Gen. Wesley Clark, Democratic
presidential candidate

This president is a miserable failure on foreign policy
and on the economy and he's got to be replaced.

—RICHARD GEPHARDT, U.S. CONGRESSMAN

THE RAPIER WIT OF "COMICAL ALI"

*The annals of warfare are rife with examples of caustic
taunting among combatants. (For proof, see chapter three,
"Words of War.") The Anglo-American Iraq War of 2003 was
a notable exception to this tradition—perhaps because the
conflict was so brief and one-sided. That didn't stop one Iraqi
official from getting his shots in, however. Over the course of
the month-long clash at arms, Iraq's Information Minister
Mohammed Saeed al-Sahhaf, dubbed "Comical Ali" in the
Western press, regularly and colorfully derided America's
commander in chief, George W. Bush, during his daily press
briefings. The extraordinarily personal nature of these insults—
covering everything from the president's height to his reputed
history of drug use—earned Mohammed Saeed al-Sahhaf, if
not a place in history, at least an honored place in Distory.*

The insane little dwarf, Bush.

The leader of the international criminal gang of
bastards.

63

The midget, Bush, and that Rumsfeld deserve only to be beaten with shoes by freedom-loving people everywhere.

Bush is a very stupid man. The American people are not stupid, they are very clever. I can't understand how such clever people came to elect such a stupid president.

I speak better English than this villain, Bush.

We're going to drag the drunken, junkie nose of Bush through Iraq's desert.

This criminal in the White House is a stupid criminal.

Bush doesn't even know if Spain is a republic or a kingdom. How can they follow this man?

~~~

SECOND BANANAS AND ALSO-RANS

America's vice presidents have come in for their share of invective as well. . . .

A labor-baiting, poker-playing, whiskey-drinking evil old man.

— JOHN L. LEWIS, U.S. LABOR LEADER, ON JOHN NANCE GARNER

He was a muddled, totally irrational man, almost incapable of uttering a coherent sentence. He was also the bitterest man I have ever encountered.

— HARRY S TRUMAN ON HIS PREDECESSOR AS VICE PRESIDENT, HENRY WALLACE

Much of what Mr. Wallace calls his global thinking is, no matter how you slice it, still Globaloney.

— CLARE BOOTH LUCE, U.S. CONGRESSWOMAN, ON HENRY WALLACE

A treacherous brain-damaged old vulture. . . . They don't hardly make 'em like Hubert any more—but just to be on the safe side, he should be castrated anyway.

— HUNTER S. THOMPSON, U.S. JOURNALIST, ON HUBERT HUMPHREY

Senator, I served with Jack Kennedy. I knew Jack Kennedy. Jack Kennedy was a friend of mine.

Senator, you're no Jack Kennedy.

—DEMOCRATIC VICE PRESIDENTIAL CANDIDATE
LLOYD BENTSEN TO HIS REPUBLICAN
COUNTERPART, DAN QUAYLE, DURING A
TELEVISED DEBATE, 1988

An empty suit that goes to funerals and plays golf.
—H. ROSS PEROT ON DAN QUAYLE

That's got every fire hydrant in America worried.
—BILL CLINTON RESPONDING TO DAN
QUAYLE'S STATED INTENTION TO BE A "PIT
BULL" DURING THE 1992 PRESIDENTIAL
CAMPAIGN

The man dyes his hair. What does that tell you about
him? He doesn't know who he is.
—GEORGE W. BUSH, ON AL GORE

. . . as have its failed presidential candidates . . .

The country does not deserve a visitation of that
potbellied, mutton-headed cucumber.
—HORACE GREELEY, ON LEWIS CASS

Grant was not fit to be nominated, and Greeley is not fit to be elected.

—JAMES A. GARFIELD ON HORACE GREELEY

One could drive a schooner through any part of his argument and never scrape against a fact.

—DAVID HOUSTON, U.S. SECRETARY OF
AGRICULTURE, ON WILLIAM JENNINGS
BRYAN

His mind was like a soup dish, wide and shallow; it could hold a small amount of nearly anything, but the slightest jarring spilled the soup into somebody's lap.

—IRVING STONE, U.S. AUTHOR, ON WILLIAM
JENNINGS BRYAN

What a disgusting, dishonest fakir Bryan is! When I see so many Americans running after him, I feel very much as I do when a really lovely woman falls in love with a cad.

—ELIHU ROOT, U.S. STATESMAN, ON WILLIAM
JENNINGS BRYAN

A kindly man and well meaning in a weak kind of way.
 —Theodore Roosevelt on William
  Jennings Bryan

A half-baked glib little briefless jackleg lawyer.
 —John Hay, U.S. secretary of state, on
  William Jennings Bryan

If you vote for Al Smith, you're voting against Christ, and you'll all be damned.
 —Mordecai Ham, U.S. Baptist revival
  leader, on Al Smith

A simple barefoot Wall Street lawyer.
 —Harold L. Ickes, U.S. presidential aide,
  on Wendell Willkie

Adlai Stevenson was a man who could never make up his mind whether he had to go to the bathroom or not.
 —Harry S Truman

It was hard to listen to Goldwater and realize that a man could be half Jewish and yet sometimes appear twice as dense as the normal Gentile.

—I. F. STONE, U.S. JOURNALIST, ON BARRY GOLDWATER

When he does smile, he looks as if he's just evicted a widow.

—MIKE ROYKO, U.S. NEWSPAPER COLUMNIST, ON BOB DOLE

The hustler from Chicago.

—GEORGE H. W. BUSH, ON JESSE JACKSON

Occasionally one also-ran even rips into another. . . .

Senator Goldwater would have been a great success in the movies—working for Eighteenth Century Fox.

—HUBERT HUMPHREY

Hubert Humphrey talks so fast that listening to him is like trying to read *Playboy* magazine with your wife turning the pages.

—BARRY GOLDWATER

DEWEY HATE HIM AND HOW

For whatever reason, twice-defeated 1944 and 1948
Republican nominee Thomas E. Dewey seems to have
elicited the most—or at least the most memorable—insults.
Perhaps it was the Snidely Whiplash moustache. . . .

He is just about the nastiest little man I've ever
known. He struts sitting down.
—LILLIAN DYKSTRA, U.S. ACADEMIC

Like the little man on top of the wedding cake.
—ATTRIBUTED TO VARIOUS SOURCES

You really have to get to know him to dislike him.
—JAMES T. PATTERSON, U.S. CONGRESSMAN

Dewey has thrown his diaper into the ring.

He is small and insignificant and he makes too much
of an effort, with his forced smile and jovial manner,
to impress himself upon people. To me he is a

political streetwalker accosting men with "come home with me, dear."

He's the only man able to walk under a bed without hitting his head.
—WALTER WINCHELL, U.S. JOURNALIST

You can't make a soufflé rise twice.
—ALICE ROOSEVELT LONGWORTH, DAUGHTER
OF THEODORE ROOSEVELT, ON DEWEY'S
SECOND RUN FOR THE WHITE HOUSE

Presidential aides and cabinet secretaries have traditionally tried to keep a low profile. Every now and then one of them rises out the White House rabbit warren and becomes a target. . . .

A worm preying on the vitals of the administration.
—JOHN QUINCY ADAMS, ON SECRETARY OF
THE TREASURY WILLIAM CRAWFORD

A dirty abolitionist sneak.

—MARY TODD LINCOLN, FIRST LADY, ON
SECRETARY OF STATE WILLIAM HENRY
SEWARD

The most garrulous old woman you were ever
annoyed by.

—GEORGE B. MCCLELLAN, U.S. GENERAL, ON
SECRETARY OF THE NAVY GIDEON WELLES

He was no better than the common cold.

—HARRY S TRUMAN, ON HAROLD L. ICKES,
AN AIDE TO HIS PREDECESSOR, FRANKLIN D.
ROOSEVELT

I watch his smart-aleck manner and his British
clothes and that New Dealism, everlasting New
Dealism in everything he says and does, and I want
to shout "Get out, get out. You stand for everything
that has been wrong with the United States for
years."

—HUGH BUTLER, U.S. SENATOR, ON
SECRETARY OF STATE DEAN ACHESON

Smooth is an inadequate word for Dulles. His prevarications are so highly polished as to be aesthetically pleasurable.

—I. F. Stone, U.S. journalist, on Secretary of State John Foster Dulles

He's thin as piss on a hot rock.

—William E. Jenner, U.S. senator, on W. Averell Harriman, U.S. diplomat

A left-leaning marshmallow.

—Bob Dole, on Attorney General Ramsey Clark

I'm glad to know the place I used to shit will be Henry's office.

—Bryce Harlow, aide to President Richard Nixon, after National Security Adviser Henry Kissinger commandeered his bathroom in order to expand his White House office.

> *And as for Confederate officials, well, the white glove slapped in an enemy's face was not the only way of settling scores in the old South. . . .*

He is as ambitious as Lucifer, cold as a snake, and what he touches will not prosper.
—SAM HOUSTON ON JEFFERSON DAVIS

Never have I seen so small a nubbin come out of so much husk.
—ABRAHAM LINCOLN ON ALEXANDER STEPHENS, CONFEDERATE VICE PRESIDENT, WHO WEIGHED ONLY ABOUT ONE HUNDRED POUNDS

CONTEMPT OF CONGRESS

No American institution can match the U.S. Congress for the amount of verbiage it produces each year. Hidden in the memoirs and papers of our elected representatives, not to mention the Congressional record, are many fine examples of cutting wit—and a few not so fine ones, perhaps validating nineteenth-century Speaker of the House Thomas Reed's famous remark about congressmen: "They never open their

74

mouths without subtracting from the sum of human knowledge."

RANDOLPH OF ROANOKE

One of the early masters of American political insult was John Randolph, an eccentric Virginia legislator who claimed Pocahontas among his forbears. An accomplished orator, Randolph was also, in the words of historian Dumas Malone, "a merciless castigator of iniquity." For most of his public career Randolph served as a leader of the opposition—to both Jeffersonians and Federalists. The adversarial role suited him well. Here are a few flashes of "Randolph of Roanoke's" trademark caustic wit. . . .

Like rotten mackerel by moonlight, he shines and stinks.
   —ON JURIST/STATESMAN EDWARD
      LIVINGSTONE

Never has ability so below mediocrity been so well rewarded. No, not even when Caligula's horse was made a consul.
   —ON SECRETARY OF THE TREASURY RICHARD
      RUSH

75

> Mr. Speaker! I mean Mr. President of the Senate and
> would-be President of the United States, which God
> in His infinite mercy avert.
>
> —TO JOHN C. CALHOUN, U.S. POLITICIAN

> You pride yourself upon an animal faculty, in respect
> to which the slave is your equal and the jackass
> infinitely your superior.
>
> —TO TRISTAM BURGES, U.S. CONGRESSMAN

*On at least one occasion, the target of one of Randolph's
tongue-lashings appears to have gotten the better of
him. . . .*

> I rejoice that the Father of Lies can never become a
> Father of Liars. One adversary of God and man is
> enough for one universe.
>
> —TRISTAM BURGES, ON RUMORS THAT
>   RANDOLPH WAS IMPOTENT

BIZARRE HATE TRIANGLE

*Henry hates John. John abhors Henry. Andrew can't stand
Henry or John—and neither of them have any use for*

Andrew. It may sound like the plot outline to a particularly lurid soap opera, but it actually describes the mutual animosity society that existed among President Andrew Jackson, his Whig nemesis Henry Clay of Kentucky, and his erstwhile ally John C. Calhoun of South Carolina. Today they are remembered as three of the giants of nineteenth-century American statecraft, but you wouldn't know it from the way they talked about one another. . . .

The Judas of the West.

He is certainly the basest, meanest scoundrel that ever disgraced the image of God, nothing is too mean or low for him to condescend to.

—ANDREW JACKSON ON HENRY CLAY

He is a bad man, an imposter, a creator of wicked schemes.
—JOHN C. CALHOUN, ON HENRY CLAY

A rigid, fanatic, ambitious, selfish partisan, and sectional turncoat with too much genius and too little common sense, who will either die a traitor or a madman.

    —HENRY CLAY, ON JOHN C. CALHOUN

Hang him as high as Haman.

    —ANDREW JACKSON, ON JOHN C. CALHOUN

I didn't shoot Henry Clay and I didn't hang John Calhoun.

    —ANDREW JACKSON, ON THINGS HE HAD LEFT UNDONE

Clay certainly elicited strong reactions—even among his friends. Here's John Quincy Adams on the man he named secretary of state in 1825. . . .

He is, like almost all the eminent men of this country, only half educated. His morals, public and private, are loose.

    —JOHN QUINCY ADAMS, ON HENRY CLAY

John Quincy had little use for another man considered one of the titans of the Senate. . . .

The gigantic intellect, the envious temper, the ravenous ambition, and the rotten heart of Daniel Webster.

    —JOHN QUINCY ADAMS

These Founding Fathers of calumny set a high standard for the generations that followed theirs on Capitol Hill. Let the roll call of insults begin. . . .

The greatest of all humbugs.

    —JOHN C. CALHOUN, ON THOMAS HART
    BENTON, U.S. SENATOR

A liar of magnitude.

    —JOHN QUINCY ADAMS, ON THOMAS HART
    BENTON

Douglas never can be president, sir. His legs are too short, sir. His coat, like a cow's tail, hangs too near the ground, sir.

    —THOMAS HART BENTON, ON STEPHEN A.
    DOUGLAS

[He] had the air and aspect of a half-naked pugilist.
—John Quincy Adams, on Stephen A. Douglas's speaking style

His argument is as thin as the . . . soup that was made by boiling the shadow of a pigeon that had been starved to death.
—Abraham Lincoln, on Stephen A. Douglas

As long as he has hope of being taken up as a candidate for the presidency he will humble himself too *low* to be respected by his party.
—R. P. Letcher, governor of Kentucky, on Stephen A. Douglas

His mind, as far as his sense of obligation to God was concerned, was a howling wilderness.
—Jeremiah Black, U.S. secretary of state, on Thaddeus Stevens, U.S. congressman

The most completely nothin' of a man that ever crossed my threshold.
—Thomas Carlyle, British historian and essayist, on Charles Summer, U.S. senator

A narrow head . . . his eyes are so close together he
can peek through a gimlet hole without blinking.

  —ULYSSES S. GRANT, ON CHARLES SUMMER,
    U.S. SENATOR

For ways that are dark
And tricks that are vain
I name Speaker Blaine
And that I dare maintain.

  —BENJAMIN F. BUTLER, U.S. CONGRESSMAN,
    ON SPEAKER OF THE HOUSE JAMES G.
    BLAINE

When Bilbo dies the epitaph on his gravestone
should read: 'Here lies Bilbo, deep in the dirt he loved
so well.'

  —PAT HARRISON, U.S. SENATOR, ON
    THEODORE BILBO, U.S. SENATOR

A degenerate son of Harvard.

  —A. LAWRENCE LOWELL, PRESIDENT OF
    HARVARD UNIVERSITY, ON HENRY CABOT
    LODGE, U.S. SENATOR

The trouble with Senator Long is that he is suffering from halitosis of the intellect. That's presuming Emperor Long has an intellect.
　—HAROLD L. ICKES, U.S. PRESIDENTIAL AIDE, ON HUEY LONG, U.S. SENATOR

He was a liar, and he was nothing but a damn demagogue. It didn't surprise me when they shot him.
　—HARRY S TRUMAN, ON HUEY LONG

He was nothing but a damn coward, and he was afraid of me.
　—HARRY S TRUMAN, ON JOSEPH McCARTHY, U.S. SENATOR

I just won't get into a pissing contest with that skunk.
　—DWIGHT D. EISENHOWER, ON JOSEPH McCARTHY

The Wizard of Ooze.
　—JOHN F. KENNEDY, ON EVERETT DIRKSEN, U.S. SENATOR

He can't talk. He's unprepossessing. And he's
generally shit.

> —JOHN F. KENNEDY, ON CARL CURTIS,
>   U.S. SENATOR

A phony. A limousine liberal, a big spender raised on
a silver spoon.

> —BOB DOLE, ON EDWARD M. KENNEDY

He was a self-important upstart and a know-it-all. . . .
[W]hen Bobby hated you, you stayed hated.

> —THOMAS P. "TIP" O'NEILL,
>   U.S. CONGRESSMAN, ON ROBERT F. KENNEDY

A taciturn, arrogant son of a bitch. . . . As far as he
was concerned, the Civil War was still going on.

> —THOMAS P. "TIP" O'NEILL, U.S.
>   CONGRESSMAN, ON HOWARD SMITH,
>   U.S. CONGRESSMAN

THE TIPPING POINT

*Speaking of "Tip" O'Neill, the corpulent longtime House
Speaker was beloved by many in his native Massachusetts
and around the country, but had his detractors as well. . . .*

The second nastiest drunk in town.
—Thomas J. Dodd, U.S. senator

He's a fat bastard.
—James Michael Curley, Boston mayor

He could be sincere and friendly when he wanted to be, but he could also turn off his charm and friendship like a light switch and become as bloodthirsty as a piranha.
—Ronald Reagan

Fat, bloated, and out of control.
—John LeBoutillier, U.S. congressman, describing "Tip" O'Neill and the federal budget

CONTROVERSIAL CONNALLY

Texas governor John Connally is best known for taking a bullet during the assassination of President John F. Kennedy. But Oswald's was not the only fire directed at the larger-than-life treasury secretary, notorious party switcher, and failed presidential candidate. During his long and eventful career, the outsize Texan won his share of brickbats. . . .

John Connally in the White House would be a
nightmare . . . when it comes between, say, ambition
and honor, it will be ambition that will win out;
when it comes between ethics and victory, ethics is
going to lose.
    —HENRY GONZALES, U.S. CONGRESSMAN

The worst, most reactionary and vicious governor in
Texas history . . . just nasty and vindictive.
    —RALPH YARBOROUGH, U.S. SENATOR

I don't like him and I don't trust him.
    —ROY WILKINS, U.S. CIVIL RIGHTS LEADER

A renegade, turncoat opportunist.
    —JOHN CONNALLY, ON JACK COX, TEXAS
       GUBERNATORIAL CANDIDATE WHO SWITCHED
       POLITICAL PARTIES FROM DEMOCRAT TO
       REPUBLICAN IN 1962 (CONNALLY HIMSELF
       MADE THE SAME SWITCH IN 1973)

Chapter Two

BATTLES OF THE BRITONS

ROYAL RIDICULE

The concept of regicide haunts the British imagination like a peckish ghost at a Scotsman's banquet table. Whether it be ambitious Macbeth snuffing out old King Duncan or the ritual sacrifice of the divine king that anchors Sir James George Frazer's classic The Golden Bough, *Britons have long dreamed of giving the ultimate what-for to their kings and queens. On one memorable occasion, they actually went through with it; for the most part, however, opponents of this or that royal personage have resorted to rhetorical assassination rather than outright violence . . .*

A most intolerable ruffian, a disgrace to human nature, and a blot of blood and grease upon the history of England.

— CHARLES DICKENS, ON HENRY VIII

A pig, an ass, a dunghill, the spawn of an adder, a basilisk, a lying buffoon, a mad fool with a frothy mouth . . . a lubberly ass . . . a frantic madman.

— MARTIN LUTHER, ON HENRY VIII

Cursed Jezebel of England!

— JOHN KNOX, SCOTTISH RELIGIOUS REFORMER, ON QUEEN MARY I

As just and merciful as Nero and as good a Christian as Mohammed.

— JOHN WESLEY, BRITISH RELIGIOUS LEADER, ON ELIZABETH I

If you do not immediately comply with my request, I will unfrock you, by God.

— ELIZABETH I TO THE BISHOP OF ELY

The most notorious whore in all the world.
—PETER WENTWORTH, MEMBER OF
PARLIAMENT, ON MARY, QUEEN OF SCOTS

OLIVER TWISTED

After Charles I was beheaded in 1649, Oliver Cromwell assumed the title of Lord Protector, along with most kingly powers. He quickly became one of the most hated men in British history, as the torrent of invective he inspired illustrates. . . .

[T]he English monster, the center of mischief, a shame to the British Chronicle, a pattern for tyranny, murder, and hypocrisy, whose bloody Caligula, Domitian, having at last attained the height of his ambition, for five years' space, he wallowed in the blood of many gallant and heroic persons . . .
—GERARD WINSTANLEY, BRITISH RADICAL

Every beast hath some evil properties; but Cromwell hath the properties of all evil beasts.
—ARCHBISHOP JOHN WILLIAMS

Cromwell wore a suit of plain cloth which seemed to have been made by an ill country tailor.

　　—ATTRIBUTED TO AN UNNAMED MEMBER OF
　　　PARLIAMENT

He lived a hypocrite and died a traitor.

　　—JOHN FOSTER, BRITISH CLERGYMAN

For better or worse, the monarchy was restored in 1660, and Britons went back to insulting their hereditary rulers. . . .

No man in England would take away my life to make you king.

　　—CHARLES II TO HIS BROTHER THE DUKE OF
　　　YORK

Here lies our mutton-loving King.
Whose word no man relies on.
Who never said a foolish thing,
And never did a wise one.

　　—THE EARL OF ROCHESTER, ON CHARLES II

I am afraid that we must expect things to go from bad to worse in England so long as a woman is in charge.

　　—PRINCE EUGENE OF SAVOY, ON QUEEN ANNE

An honest blockhead.
  —LADY MARY WORTLEY MONTAGU,
    ON GEORGE I

Who's your fat friend?
  —GEORGE BRYAN "BEAU" BRUMMELL,
    ENGLISH DANDY, REFERRING TO GEORGE,
    PRINCE OF WALES (LATER KING GEORGE IV)

A more contemptible, cowardly, selfish, unfeeling dog
does not exist than this king.
  —CHARLES GREVILLE, BRITISH DIARIST,
    ON KING GEORGE IV

Nowadays a parlor maid as ignorant as Queen
Victoria was when she came to the throne would be
classed as mentally defective.
  —GEORGE BERNARD SHAW

She's more of a man than I expected.
  —HENRY JAMES, U.S. NOVELIST,
    ON QUEEN VICTORIA

A corpulent voluptuary.
  —RUDYARD KIPLING, ON EDWARD VII

> I'm prepared to take advice on leisure from Prince
> Philip. He's a world expert on leisure. He's been
> practicing for most of his adult life.
> —Neil Kinnock, Labour politician, on
> the Duke of Edinburgh

> She is a lady short on looks, absolutely deprived of
> any sense, has a figure like a Jurassic monster, very
> greedy when it comes to loot, no tact, and wants to
> upstage everyone else.
> —Sir Nicholas Fairbairn, Conservative
> politician, on Sarah Ferguson,
> Duchess of York

PRIME MINISTER, PRIME TARGET

*For a nation that prides itself on civility and deference,
Great Britain has elected more than its fair share of divisive
prime ministers. Gladstone and Thatcher are just two of the
Downing Street inhabitants to provoke a visceral dislike
among political rivals and certain portions of the electorate.
While not all PMs can match the volume of vituperation
these two leaders inspired, few in the modern era have left
office without having at least a few insults lobbed their way.*

SIR ROBERT WALPOLE (1721–1742)

He would do mean things for profit, and never thought of doing great ones for glory.
　　—LORD CHESTERFIELD, BRITISH STATESMAN

GEORGE GRENVILLE (1763–1765)

A fatiguing orator and indefatigable drudge; more likely to disgust than offend.
　　—HORACE WALPOLE, BRITISH WRITER AND
　　ANTIQUARIAN

HENRY ADDINGTON (1801–1804)

The indefinable air of a village apothecary inspecting the tongue of the state.
　　—LORD ARCHIBALD ROSEBERY

ROBERT BANKS JENKINSON (1812–1827)

[He] has acted as he always does to a friend in personal questions—shabbily, timidly, and ill.
　　—LORD PALMERSTON

SIR ROBERT PEEL (1834–1835, 1841–1846)

The right honorable gentleman is reminiscent of a poker. The only difference is that a poker gives off the occasional signs of warmth.

The right honourable gentlemen's smile is like the silver fittings of a coffin.

—BENJAMIN DISRAELI

LORD JOHN RUSSELL (1846–1852, 1865–1866)

If a traveler were informed that such a man was the leader of the House of Commons, he might begin to comprehend how the Egyptians worshiped an insect.

—BENJAMIN DISRAELI

LORD PALMERSTON (1855–1858, 1859–1865)

Your Lordship is like a favorite footman on easy terms with his mistress. Your dexterity seems a happy compound of the smartness of an attorney's clerk and the intrigue of a Greek of the lower empire.

    —BENJAMIN DISRAELI

We had, God knows, terrible trouble with him about foreign affairs . . . I never liked him.

    —QUEEN VICTORIA

His administration at the Foreign Office was one long crime.

    —JOHN BRIGHT, LIBERAL POLITICIAN

BENJAMIN DISRAELI (1868, 1874–1880)

He is a self-made man and worships his creator.

    —JOHN BRIGHT, LIBERAL POLITICIAN

He is not such a Turk as I thought. What he hates is Christian liberty and reconstruction.

    —WILLIAM GLADSTONE

He is the most degraded of his species and kind; and England is degraded in tolerating or having upon the face of her society a miscreant of his abominable, foul, and atrocious nature.

—DANIEL O'CONNELL, IRISH POLITICIAN

How long will John Bull allow this absurd monkey to dance on his chest?

—THOMAS CARLYLE, BRITISH HISTORIAN AND ESSAYIST

He had a complete and almost proverbial lack of political principle, often acting by instinct.

—HAROLD WILSON

WILLIAM E. GLADSTONE (1868–1874, 1880–1885, 1886, 1892–1894)

Mr. Gladstone speaks to me as if I were a public meeting.

—QUEEN VICTORIA

The danger to the country, to Europe, to her vast Empire, which is involved in having all these great interests entrusted to the shaking hand of an old, wild, and incomprehensible man of eighty-two and a half, is very great!

—QUEEN VICTORIA, REACTING TO
GLADSTONE'S FOURTH AND LAST
APPOINTMENT AS PRIME MINISTER IN 1892

One of the contemptiblest men I ever looked on. A poor ritualist; an almost spectral kind of phantasm of a man.

—THOMAS CARLYLE, BRITISH HISTORIAN AND
ESSAYIST

A sophisticated rhetorician, inebriated with the exuberance of his own verbosity, and gifted with an egotistical imagination that can at all times command an interminable and inconsistent series of arguments to malign an opponent and to glorify himself.

That unprincipled maniac.

If Gladstone fell into the Thames, it would be a misfortune. But if someone pulled him out, it would be a calamity.

He has not one single redeeming defect.

He was essentially a prig, and among prigs there is a Freemasonry which never fails. All the prigs spoke of him as the coming man.

He made his conscience not his guide but his accomplice.

—BENJAMIN DISRAELI

He was generally thought be very pusillanimous in dealing with foreign affairs. That is not at all the impression I derived. He was wholly ignorant.
—LORD EVELYN CROMER,
BRITISH ADMINISTRATOR

I don't object to the Old Man's always having the ace of trumps up his sleeve, but merely to his belief that God Almighty put it there.
—HENRY LABOUCHERE, LIBERAL POLITICIAN

God must be very angry with England when he sends back Mr. Gladstone to us as first minister.
   —VISCOUNT WOLSELEY, BRITISH FIELD
      MARSHAL

Mr. Gladstone read Homer for fun, which I thought served him right.
   —WINSTON CHURCHILL

LORD SALISBURY (1885–1886, 1886–1892, 1895–1901)

That strange powerful inscrutable and brilliant obstructive deadweight at the top.
   —LORD CURZON, CONSERVATIVE POLITICIAN

His face is livid, gaunt his white body, his breath is green with gall; his tongue drips poison.
   —JOHN QUINCY ADAMS, U.S. PRESIDENT

ARTHUR J. BALFOUR (1902–1905)

His impact on history would be no more than the whiff of scent on a lady's handkerchief.
   —DAVID LLOYD GEORGE

SIR HENRY CAMPBELL BANNERMAN (1905–1908)

He is a mere cork, dancing in a current which he cannot control.
—ARTHUR BALFOUR

HERBERT H. ASQUITH (1908–1916)

Black and wicked and with only a nodding acquaintance with the truth.
—LADY CUNARD, SOCIALITE AND HEIRESS

When one has peeled off the brown-paper wrapping of phrases and compromises, one finds—just nothing at all.
—LYTTON STRACHEY, BIOGRAPHER AND CRITIC

DAVID LLOYD GEORGE (1916–1922)

Oh, if I could piss the way he speaks!
—GEORGES CLEMENCEAU, FRENCH PRIME MINISTER

He couldn't see a belt without hitting below it.
  —MARGOT ASQUITH, WIFE OF PRIME
    MINISTER HERBERT ASQUITH

My one ardent desire is that after the war he should
be publicly castrated in front of Nurse Cavell's statue.
  —LYTTON STRACHEY, BRITISH WRITER

He did not care in which direction the car was
traveling, so long as he remained in the driver's seat.
  —LORD BEAVERBROOK

He spent his whole life in plastering together the true
and the false and therefrom manufacturing the
plausible.

He is a mere shadow of his former self, wandering in a
sort of Celtic twilight, his only intention being to rob
hen roosts.

  —STANLEY BALDWIN, BRITISH STATESMAN

The Happy Warrior of Squandermania.
—Winston Churchill

It's a waste of time explaining strategy to you. To understand my explanation you would have had to have my experience.
—Sir William Robertson, chief of the Imperial General Staff

ANDREW BONAR LAW (1922–1923)

It is fitting that we should have buried the Unknown Prime Minister by the side of the Unknown Soldier.
—Herbert Asquith

He was honest to the point of simplicity.
—David Lloyd George

STANLEY BALDWIN (1923–1924, 1924–1929, 1935–1937)

I think Baldwin has gone mad. He simply takes one jump in the dark; looks around and then takes another.
—Lord Birkenhead, Conservative politician

One could not even dignify him with the name of stuffed shirt. He was simply a hole in the air.

—GEORGE ORWELL

I wish Stanley Baldwin no ill, but it would have been much better if he had never lived.

An epileptic corpse. Occasionally he stumbled over the truth, but hastily picked himself up and hurried on as if nothing had happened.

—WINSTON CHURCHILL

A mixture of innocence, ignorance, honesty, and stupidity . . . He is a man of the utmost insignificance.

Baldwin's evil geniuses are the whippersnappers of the Cabinet, Amery and Chamberlain. They buzz about him day and night and he is lamentably weak.

—LORD CURZON, CONSERVATIVE POLITICIAN

> He was the finely tuned manipulator of the steering wheel: direction without engine power, the prerogative of the bosun throughout the ages.
> —HAROLD WILSON

The candle in that great turnip has gone out.
—WINSTON CHURCHILL, UPON HEARING THAT
BALDWIN HAD DIED

JAMES RAMSAY MACDONALD (1924–1935)

He has sufficient conscience to bother him, but not sufficient to keep him straight.
—DAVID LLOYD GEORGE

We know that he has, more than any other man, the gift of compressing the largest amount of words into the smallest amount of thought.

I remember, when I was a child, being taken to the celebrated Barnum's Circus which contained an exhibition of freaks and monstrosities. The exhibit on the program which I most desired to see was the one described as The Boneless Wonder. My parents judged that the spectacle would be too revolting and demoralizing for my youthful eyes and I have waited fifty years to see the boneless wonder sitting opposite on the treasury bench.

—WINSTON CHURCHILL

A pathetic figure—tired, ill, rambling, and taking refuge in virtually meaningless and almost unending phrases.
—HAROLD WILSON

NEVILLE CHAMBERLAIN (1937–1940)

The people of Birmingham have a specially heavy burden for they have given the world the curse of the present British Prime Minister.
—SIR STAFFORD CRIPPS, LABOUR POLITICIAN

He saw foreign policy through the wrong end of a municipal drainpipe.

A retail mind in a wholesale business.

Look at his head. The worst thing Neville Chamberlain ever did was to meet Hitler and let Hitler see him.

—DAVID LLOYD GEORGE

At the depths of that dusty soul there is nothing but abject surrender.
—WINSTON CHURCHILL

Chamberlain is no better than a Mayor of Birmingham, and in a lean year at that.
—LORD HUGH CECIL

The worst thing I can say about democracy is that it has tolerated the right honorable gentleman for four and half years.

Listening to a speech by Chamberlain is like paying a visit to Woolworth's. Everything in its place and nothing above sixpence.

He has the lucidity which is the byproduct of a fundamentally sterile mind.

—ANEURIN BEVAN, LABOUR POLITICIAN

You have sat too long here for any good you have been doing. Depart, I say, and let us have done with you. In the name of God, *go!*
—LEOPOLD CHARLES MAURICE STENNETT AMERY, TO NEVILLE CHAMBERLAIN, IN A SPEECH IN THE HOUSE OF COMMONS, MAY 1940

WINSTON CHURCHILL (1940–1945, 1951–1955)

I thought he was a young man of promise; but it appears he was a young man of promises.
—ARTHUR BALFOUR

> He is a military adventurer who would sell his sword to anyone. He has his sentimental side but he lacks soul.

When Winston was born lots of fairies swooped down on his cradle with gifts: imagination, eloquence, industry, ability; and then came a fairy who said, "No one person has the right to so many gifts," picked him up and gave him such a shake and twist that with all the gifts he was denied judgment and wisdom.

—STANLEY BALDWIN

Winston, if I were your wife, I would put poison in your coffee.

Nancy, if I were your husband, I would drink it.

—A CONVERSATION BETWEEN CHURCHILL AND CONSERVATIVE POLITICIAN NANCY ASTOR

Winston, you're drunk!

Bessie, you're ugly. And tomorrow morning I shall be sober.

—A CONVERSATION BETWEEN CHURCHILL AND LABOUR POLITICIAN BESSIE BRADDOCK

Churchill has the habit of breaking the rungs of any ladder he puts his foot to.

Churchill on top of the wave has in him the stuff of which tyrants are made.

—LORD BEAVERBROOK

He is a man suffering from petrified adolescence.

He never spares himself in conversation. He gives himself so generously that hardly anybody else is permitted to give anything in his presence.

—ANEURIN BEVAN, LABOUR POLITICIAN

He would kill his own mother just so that he could use her skin to make a drum to beat his own praises.

—MARGOT ASQUITH, WIFE OF PRIME MINISTER HERBERT ASQUITH

Fifty percent of Winston is genius, 50 percent bloody fool. He will behave like a child.

—CLEMENT ATTLEE

Winston has devoted the best years of his life to preparing his impromptu speeches.

—LORD BIRKENHEAD, CONSERVATIVE POLITICIAN

Simply a radio personality who outlived his prime.

—EVELYN WAUGH, BRITISH NOVELIST

I am enclosing two tickets to the first night of my new play, bring a friend—if you have one.

> —GEORGE BERNARD SHAW, IN A LETTER TO CHURCHILL

Cannot possibly attend first night, will attend second—if there is one.

> —WINSTON CHURCHILL, IN REPLY

CLEMENT ATTLEE (1945–1951)

A tardy little marionette.

> —RANDOLPH CHURCHILL

An empty taxi arrived at 10 Downing Street, and when the door was opened, Attlee got out.

A modest man, who has much to be modest about.

He is a sheep in sheep's clothing.

> —WINSTON CHURCHILL

> "He seems determined to make a trumpet sound like a tin whistle. He brings to the fierce struggle of politics the tepid enthusiasm of a lazy summer afternoon at a cricket match."
>
> —ANEURIN BEVAN, LABOUR POLITICIAN

ANTHONY EDEN (1955–1957)

He is not only a bore, but he bores England.
> —MALCOM MUGGERIDGE, BRITISH AUTHOR

Not a gentleman. Dresses too well.
> —BERTRAND RUSSELL, BRITISH PHILOSOPHER

The juvenile lead.
> —ANEURIN BEVAN, LABOUR POLITICIAN

An overripe banana, yellow outside, squishy in.
> —REGINALD PAGET, LABOUR POLITICIAN

Well, he is the best Prime Minister we have.
> —RICHARD AUSTEN BUTLER, CONSERVATIVE
> POLITICIAN, ON BEING ASKED IF HE
> SUPPORTED EDEN

There is no reason to attack the monkey when the organ-grinder is present.

> —ANEURIN BEVAN, LABOUR POLITICIAN,
> REFERRING TO CHANCELLOR OF THE
> EXCHEQUER SELWYN LLOYD AND
> MACMILLAN, RESPECTIVELY

The Prime Minister has an absolute genius for putting flamboyant labels on empty luggage.

> —ANEURIN BEVAN, LABOUR POLITICIAN

He has inherited the streak of charlatanry in Disraeli without his vision, and the self-righteousness of Gladstone without his dedication to principle.

He had an expensive education—Eton and Suez.

> —HAROLD WILSON

ALEC DOUGLAS-HOME (1963–1964)

> After half a century of democratic advance, the whole process has ground to a halt with a Fourteenth Earl.
> —HAROLD WILSON

An amiable enough creature—however, I am afraid he doesn't understand economics or even education at all.
> —RICHARD AUSTEN BUTLER, CONSERVATIVE POLITICIAN

HAROLD WILSON (1964–1970, 1974–1976)

If ever he went to school without any boots it was because he was too big for them.
> —IVOR BULMER-THOMAS,
> BRITISH CHURCHMAN

Harold Wilson had one overriding aim—to remain in office. He would use almost every trick or gimmick to achieve it. Whenever I go to see Harold, I look into those gray eyes—and see nothing.
> —RICHARD CROSSMAN, LABOUR POLITICIAN

He was adept at using the smear as a political weapon.

   —RICHARD AUSTEN BUTLER,
     CONSERVATIVE POLITICIAN

He did not have political principle. He had no sense of direction and rarely looked more than a few months ahead. He had short-term opportunism allied with a capacity for self-delusion, which made Walter Mitty appear unimaginative.

   —DENIS HEALEY, LABOUR POLITICIAN

EDWARD HEATH (1970–1974)

A shiver looking for a spine to run up.

   —HAROLD WILSON

The Incredible Sulk.

   —GREG KNIGHT, CONSERVATIVE POLITICIAN

JAMES CALLAGHAN (1976–1979)

He was skillful in debate, persuasive in speech—and disastrous at his job.

   —LORD WYATT, LABOUR POLITICIAN

He presided over debt, drift, and decay.
  —MARGARET THATCHER

MARGARET THATCHER (1979–1990)

She probably thinks Sinai is the plural of sinus.
  —JONATHAN AITKEN, CONSERVATIVE
  POLITICIAN

She has the mouth of Marilyn Monroe and the eyes
of Caligula.
  —FRANCOIS MITTERRAND, FRENCH PRESIDENT

She approaches the problems of our country with all
the one-dimensional subtlety of a comic strip.

Margaret Thatcher says that she has given the French
president a piece of her mind—this is not a gift I
would receive with alacrity.

  —DENIS HEALEY, LABOUR POLITICIAN

She'll probably replace Guy Fawkes as an effigy.
    —KEN LIVINGSTONE, LABOUR POLITICIAN

She is about as environmentally friendly as the bubonic plague. I would be happy to see [her] stuffed, mounted, put in a glass case, and left in a museum.

A half-mad old bag lady.

    —TONY BANKS, LABOUR POLITICIAN

JOHN MAJOR (1990–1997)

A Thatcherite with a grin. He deserved to be called Tinkerbell as all he did was tinker with the problems of the British economy.
    —TONY BANKS, LABOUR POLITICIAN

I wouldn't spit in their mouths if their teeth were on fire.

—RODNEY BICKERSTAFFE, BRITISH LABOR LEADER, REFERRING TO MAJOR AND HIS CHANCELLOR OF THE EXCHEQUER NORMAN LAMONT

More a ventriloquist's dummy than a Prime Minister.

—SIR NICHOLAS FAIRBAIRN, CONSERVATIVE POLITICIAN

John Major is what he is: a man from nowhere, going nowhere, heading for a well-merited obscurity as fast as his mediocre talents can carry him.

—PAUL JOHNSON, BRITISH HISTORIAN

Napoleon in his first one hundred days recaptured Paris without a battle. John Major in his first one hundred days buried Thatcherism without a tear. Thereafter, they were both destroyed for their previous misdeeds.

—MICHAEL FOOT, LABOUR POLITICIAN

The thing about Mrs. Thatcher was there was a character to assassinate. The problem with Mr. Major is that you look and look—and where is it?

—GERALD KAUFMAN, LABOUR POLITICIAN

He presided over the most wasteful, inefficient, and incompetent government in living memory. . . . Major pretends he has no responsibility for the state of the nation he has governed. It's as if he had just landed from Mars.

—TONY BLAIR

TONY BLAIR (1997–)

He appears to have no clear political view except that the world should be a nicer place and that he should be loved and trusted by everyone and questioned by no one.

—NORMAN BERESFORD TEBBIT, LORD TEBBIT, CONSERVATIVE POLITICIAN

He's so vain he'd take his own hand in marriage.

—GREG KNIGHT, CONSERVATIVE POLITICIAN

He is sanctimonious and cloaks himself in righteousness.
—JOHN MAJOR

In just one year, a man with confident early pledges has become full of meaningless waffle.
—WILLIAM HAGUE, CONSERVATIVE PARTY LEADER

He is a man who has no single political principle within him, who will change his views as often as opinion polls and spin doctors tell him to.
—JOHN REDWOOD, CONSERVATIVE POLITICIAN

PARLIAMENTARY PUT-DOWNS

Steady erosion of the powers of the crown brought with it a more robust role for the Houses of Parliament. This raised the stakes considerably. No longer required simply to rubber-stamp the edicts of a king, MPs now had a major say in the governing of an empire. That led to more spirited Parliamentary debate and, as anyone who has watched the

House of Commons proceedings in person or on TV can attest,
a raucous atmosphere conducive to the exchange of insults. . . .

The most popular man, and the most able to do hurt, that hath lived in any time.
 —EDWARD HYDE, EARL OF CLARENDON, ON JOHN PYM, ANTIROYALIST MEMBER OF PARLIAMENT

A parson in a tie-wig.
 —BERNARD MANDEVILLE, BRITISH DOCTOR AND WIT, ON WHIG POLITICIAN JOSEPH ADDISON

LORD SANDWICH: You will die either on the gallows, or of the pox.

JOHN WILKES: That must depend on whether I embrace your lordship's principles or your mistress.

Burke was a damned wrong-headed fellow, through his whole life jealous and obstinate.
 —CHARLES JAMES FOX, BRITISH WHIG POLITICIAN, ON EDMUND BURKE

Lord Shaftesbury would have been in a lunatic asylum if he had not devoted himself to reforming lunatic asylums.

—FLORENCE NIGHTINGALE, BRITISH NURSING PIONEER, ON LORD SHAFTESBURY, CONSERVATIVE POLITICIAN

The right honorable gentleman is indebted to his memory for his jests and to his imagination for his facts.

—RICHARD BRINSLEY SHERIDAN, WHIG POLITICIAN, ON THE EARL OF DUMAS

He is at once a tyrant, a trickster, a visionary, and a deceiver . . . he reasons in bombast, prevaricates in metaphor, and quibbles in heroics.

—RICHARD BRINSLEY SHERIDAN, WHIG POLITICIAN, ON WARREN HASTINGS, GOVERNOR-GENERAL OF INDIA

[H]e insults the House of Lords and plagues the most eminent of his colleagues with the crabbed malice of a maundering witch.

—BENJAMIN DISRAELI, ON THE EARL OF ABERDEEN

The most conceited person with whom I have ever
been brought in contact.
   —BENJAMIN DISRAELI, ON CHARLES
      GREVILLE, DIARIST AND POLITICIAN

Lord Birkenhead is very clever, but sometimes his
brains go to his head.
   —MARGOT ASQUITH, WIFE OF PRIME
      MINISTER HERBERT ASQUITH, ON FREDERICK
      SMITH, LORD BIRKENHEAD, A MEMBER OF
      HER HUSBAND'S CABINET

A man with the vision of an eagle but with a blind
spot in his eye.
   —ANDREW BONAR LAW, ON LORD BIRKENHEAD

Like a cushion he always bore the impress of the last
man who had sat on him.
   —DAVID LLOYD GEORGE, ON LORD DERBY,
      BRITISH MINISTER OF WAR DURING
      WORLD WAR I

The right honorable and learned gentleman has twice crossed the floor of this House, each time leaving behind a trail of slime.

> —DAVID LLOYD GEORGE, ON SIR JOHN SIMON,
>   LIBERAL POLITICIAN

He was a mean man . . . I am glad I trampled upon his carcass. He would have pursued me even from his grave.

> —DAVID LLOYD GEORGE, ON EDWARD GREY,
>   LIBERAL POLITICIAN

Simon has sat on the fence so long that the iron has entered his soul.

> —DAVID LLOYD GEORGE, ON JOHN
>   ALLSEBROOK SIMON, LIBERAL POLITICIAN

I met Curzon in Downing Street, from whom I got the sort of greeting a corpse would give to an undertaker.

> —STANLEY BALDWIN, ON LORD CURZON,
>   CONSERVATIVE POLITICIAN

In the old days I suppose I should have called him out and shot him like a dog for his grossly insulting letter.
—EARL KITCHENER, BRITISH GENERAL, ON LORD CURZON, CONSERVATIVE POLITICIAN

We will support Henderson as a rope supports a man who is hanged.
—VLADIMIR ILYICH LENIN, ON ARTHUR HENDERSON, LABOUR POLITICIAN

A curious mixture of geniality and venom.
—WINSTON CHURCHILL, ON HERBERT MORRISON, LABOUR POLITICIAN

He is one of those orators of whom it was well said, "Before they get up they do not know what they are going to say; when they are speaking, they do not know what they are saying; and when they sit down, they do not know what they have said."
—WINSTON CHURCHILL, REFERRING TO LORD CHARLES BERESFORD

> When sexual indulgence has reduced a man to the shape of Lord Hailsham, sexual continence involves no more than a sense of the ridiculous.
> —REGINALD PAGET, LABOUR POLITICIAN, ON LORD HAILSHAM, CONSERVATIVE POLITICIAN

FAIR GAME

Not even heroes like Lawrence of Arabia or Sir Walter Raleigh escape the lash of the British insult. And as for Irish nationalists, well, they're always ripe for slamming. . . .

> Thou art the most vile and execrable traitor that ever lived . . . thy name is hateful to all the realm of England. . . . There never lived a viler viper upon the face of the earth than thou.
> —SIR EDWARD COKE, BRITISH JURIST, TO SIR WALTER RALEIGH

A bore and a bounder and a prig. He was intoxicated with his own youth, and loathed any milieu which he couldn't dominate. Certainly he had none of a

gentleman's instincts, strutting about Peace
Conferences in Arab dress.
   —Sir Henry "Chips" Channon,
      Conservative politician, on
      T. E. Lawrence

A systematic liar and a beggarly cheat; a swindler and
a poltroon. . . . He has committed every crime that
does not require courage.
   —Benjamin Disraeli, on Daniel
      O'Connell, Irish politician

The only way to deal with such a man as O'Connell
is to hang him up and erect a statue to him under the
gallows.
   —Sidney Smith, English cleric, on
      Daniel O'Connell, Irish politician

FIRST FAMILIES

*Two "royal" families dominated British politics in the half
century leading up to World War II: The Chamberlains
(father Joseph and sons Austen and Neville) and the*

Churchills (father Randolph and son Winston). Despite their immense contributions to British history they earned quite a number of brickbats—and, in Winston's case, dished out a few as well. . . .

The manners of a cad and the tongue of a bargee.
> —HERBERT ASQUITH, BRITISH PRIME
> MINISTER, ON JOSEPH CHAMBERLAIN

Mr. Chamberlain . . . looked and spoke like a cheesemonger.
> —BENJAMIN DISRAELI, ON JOSEPH
> CHAMBERLAIN

He was not born, bred, or educated in the ways which alone secure the necessary tact and behavior of a real gentleman.
> —SIR EDWARD HAMILTON, BRITISH STATESMAN,
> ON JOSEPH CHAMBERLAIN

There never was a Churchill from John of Marlborough down that had either morals or principles.
> —WILLIAM GLADSTONE, ON LORD RANDOLPH
> CHURCHILL

To have betrayed two political leaders—to have
wrecked two historic parties—reveals a depth of
infamy never previously reached, compared with
which the thugs of India are as faithful friends and
Judas Iscariot is entitled to a crown of glory.

    —JOHN BURNS, BRITISH LABOR LEADER,
      ON JOSEPH CHAMBERLAIN

Mr. Chamberlain loves the working man; he loves to
see him work.

    —WINSTON CHURCHILL, ON JOSEPH
      CHAMBERLAIN

He always played the game and he always last it.

    —WINSTON CHURCHILL, ON AUSTEN
      CHAMBERLAIN

GOOD-BYE, MR. CRIPPS

*One of the leading critics of the Churchill government
throughout World War II, Labour gadfly Sir Richard Stafford
Cripps came in for his share of abuse over the years—from
all political quarters. . . .*

Sir Stafford has a brilliant mind until it is made up.
—LADY VIOLET BONHAM-CARTER

There but for the grace of God goes God.
—WINSTON CHURCHILL, ON SEEING CRIPPS
PASS BY

Seldom has anyone's political stock, having been so outrageously and unjustifiably overvalued, fallen so fast and so far.
—HUGH DALTON, LABOUR POLITICIAN

He delivers his speech with an expression of injured guilt.

He has all the virtues I dislike and none of the vices I admire.

—WINSTON CHURCHILL

Another politician who provoked a great deal of bile was Aneurin "Nye" Bevan, the outspoken Labour firebrand who served as minister of health from 1945 to 1951. . . .

Not while I'm alive, he ain't.
 —ERNEST BEVIN, LABOUR POLITICIAN, WHEN TOLD THAT ANEURIN BEVAN WAS HIS OWN WORST ENEMY

Unless the right honorable gentleman changes his policy and methods and moves without the slightest delay, he will be as great a curse to this country in peace as he was a squalid nuisance in time of war.
 —WINSTON CHURCHILL

He enjoys prophesying the imminent fall of the capitalist system and is prepared to play a part, any part, in its burial—except that of a mute.
 —HAROLD MACMILLAN

Always a quick wit, Bevan gave as good as he got. While he reserved his best insults for Tory prime ministers (see above), he wasn't afraid to turn his cudgels on members of his own party. . . .

A squalid, backstairs, third-rate Tammany Hall politician.
—ANEURIN BEVAN, ON HERBERT MORRISON,
LABOUR POLITICIAN

A desiccated calculating machine.
—ANEURIN BEVAN, ON HUGH GAITSKELL,
LABOUR PARTY LEADER

ERA OF BAD FEELINGS

The 1980s proved to be a brief golden age of verbal venom in British politics. Labour leader Neil Kinnock and Tory gadfly Lord Tebbit always seemed to be in the center of these exchanges. . . .

He possesses an ego fat on arrogance and drunk on ambition.
—NEIL KINNOCK, LABOUR PARTY LEADER, ON
DAVID OWEN, LORD OWEN, LABOUR
POLITICIAN

A windbag whose incoherent speeches spring from an incoherent mind.

—Norman Beresford Tebbit, Lord Tebbit, Conservative politician, on Neil Kinnock, Labour party leader

A boil on a verruca.

—Neil Kinnock, Labour party leader, on Norman Beresford Tebbit, Lord Tebbit, Conservative politician

A semi house-trained polecat.

—Michael Foot, Labour politician, on Norman Beresford Tebbit, Lord Tebbit, Conservative politician

A PARTING SHOT

In recent years the level of vituperation in British politics has abated somewhat, though occasionally an especially priceless bit of venom does slip through, as in this excerpt from an exchange between two Tory MPs during a salmonella crisis in the 1980s. . . .

Does the honorable lady remember that she was an egg herself once: and very many members of all sides of this House regret that it was ever fertilized.

—SIR NICHOLAS FAIRBAIRN, CONSERVATIVE POLITICIAN, TO EDWINA CURRIE, CONSERVATIVE POLITICIAN

Chapter Three

————

WORDS OF WAR

In which we learn that not all battlefield casualties come at the point of a bayonet or a flash of shellfire. Often the verbal volleys flung at military commanders cause the deepest wounds of all. . . .

A savage old Nabob, with an immense fortune, a tawny complexion, a bad liver, and a worse heart.

—THOMAS BABINGTON MACAULAY, BRITISH
WHIG POLITICIAN, ON ROBERT CLIVE,
BRITISH STATESMAN AND GENERAL

> He seems to have been so hackneyed in villainy, and so lost to all sense of honor and shame that while his facilities will enable him to continue his sordid pursuits there will be no time for remorse.
>
> GEORGE WASHINGTON, ON BENEDICT ARNOLD

A man who habitually consults the prophet Isaiah when he is in difficulty is not apt to obey the orders of anyone.

—SIR EVELYN BARING, BRITISH
ADMINISTRATOR, ON CHARLES GEORGE
GORDON, BRITISH GENERAL

He has all the characteristics of a dog except loyalty.
—SAM HOUSTON, ON THOMAS JEFFERSON
GREEN, TEXAS GENERAL AND POLITICIAN

BONEY AND THE DUKE

No two commanders exhibited more contempt for each other than Napoleon Bonaparte and the Duke of Wellington. Still bitter following his defeat at Waterloo, the French emperor actually left money in his will to a man who had tried to assassinate Wellington. For his part, the victorious Briton

achieved a different kind of coup de grace over his erstwhile
opposite number by sleeping with two of Napoleon's
mistresses. Their war of words was equally personal. . . .

He accepted peace as if he had been defeated.
—NAPOLEON BONAPARTE, ON THE DUKE OF
WELLINGTON

Bonaparte's whole life, civil, political, and military,
was a fraud. There was not a transaction, great or
small, in which lying and fraud were not introduced.
—THE DUKE OF WELLINGTON, ON NAPOLEON
BONAPARTE

I tell you Wellington is a bad general, the English are
bad soldiers; we will settle the matter by lunchtime.
—NAPOLEON BONAPARTE, TO HIS SOLDIERS ON
THE MORNING OF THE BATTLE OF WATERLOO

I don't care a two-penny damn what becomes of the
ashes of Napoleon Bonaparte.
—THE DUKE OF WELLINGTON, ON LEARNING
OF NAPOLEON'S DEMISE AT ST. HELENA

Wellington wasn't the only person who hated Napoleon, of course. The rest of Europe couldn't stand the Little Corporal either. Even his own brother had issues. . . .

A cold-blooded, calculating, unprincipled usurper, without a virtue; no statesman, knowing nothing of commerce, political economy, or civil government, and supplying ignorance by bold presumption.
　　—THOMAS JEFFERSON, ON NAPOLEON
　　　BONAPARTE

That infernal creature who is the curse of all the human race becomes every day more and more abominable.
　　—ALEXANDER I, CZAR OF RUSSIA, IN A LETTER
　　　TO HIS SISTER CATHERINE

Napoleon is a torrent which as yet we are unable to stem. Moscow will be the sponge that will suck him dry.
　　—MIKHAIL KUTUZOV, RUSSIAN PRINCE AND
　　　MARSHAL

Napoleon is a dangerous man in a free country. He seems to me to have the makings of a tyrant, and I believe that were he to be king he would be fully capable of playing such a part, and his name would become an object of detestation to posterity and every right-minded patriot.

    —LUCIEN BONAPARTE, YOUNGER BROTHER OF
      NAPOLEON, IN A LETTER TO HIS BROTHER
      JOSEPH

UNCIVIL DISCOURSE

The American Civil War produced quite a parade of generals, particularly on the Union side. Some fought, some didn't; few made it from one end of the conflict to the other unscathed—by the insults of their colleagues and political superiors, that is. . . .

A lamentably successful cross between a fox and a hog.

    —JAMES G. BLAINE, U.S. DIPLOMAT, ON GEN.
      BENJAMIN BUTLER

Originates nothing, anticipates nothing, takes no responsibility, plans nothing, suggests nothing, is good for nothing.

    —GIDEON WELLES, U.S. SECRETARY OF THE
      NAVY, ON GEN. HENRY HALLECK

A stumpy, quadrangular little man, with a forehead of no promise and hair so short that it looks like a coat of black paint.
—GEORGE TEMPLETON STRONG, CIVIL WAR-ERA DIARIST, ON GEN. PHILIP SHERIDAN

The Attila of the American continent.
—JEFFERSON DAVIS, CONFEDERATE PRESIDENT, ON GEN. WILLIAM TECUMSEH SHERMAN

"Fighting Joe," so famous as a subordinate, bent under the strain of supreme command.
—WINSTON CHURCHILL, ON U.S. GEN. JOSEPH HOOKER

Grant still represents the butcher type of general.
—J. F. C. FULLER, U.S. GENERAL, ON ULYSSES S. GRANT

HONEST ABE LAYS THE (S)MAC DOWN

No Civil War feud can compare to the one between Abraham Lincoln and Gen. George B. McClellan. McClellan famously derided Lincoln for his simian bearing (see Spite House in chapter one), while Lincoln reserved his criticism for Little Mac's somewhat tortoise-like approach to pressing the advantage on the battlefield. Herewith a few of the railsplitter's more pointed comments about his top commander.

Major General McClellan,
I have just read your dispatch about sore-tongued and fatigued horses. Will you pardon me for asking what the horses of your army have done since the battle of Antietam that fatigues anything?
—ABRAHAM LINCOLN, IN A TELEGRAM TO
    GEN. GEORGE B. McCLELLAN

My Dear McClellan:
If you don't want to use the army I should like to borrow it for a while.
    YOURS RESPECTFULLY,
    A. LINCOLN

He is an admirable engineer, but he seems to have a special talent for a stationary engine.

I said I would remove him if he let Lee's army get away from him, and I must do so. He has got the "slows."

The stakes rose considerably with the outbreak of World War I. Now failure to execute on the battlefield could have terminal consequences for the nations involved. As a result, the level of acrimony rose accordingly. . . .

An example of the gulf that separates theory from practice. He believed in mathematics rather than in maneuver, and in number rather than in moral force.
—FERDINAND FOCH, FRENCH GENERAL, ON
HELMUTH KARL VON MOLTKE,
GERMAN GENERAL

Falkenhayn is the evil genius of our Fatherland, and, unfortunately, he has the Kaiser in his pocket.
—MAX VON HOFFMANN, GERMAN GENERAL,
ON ERICH VON FALKENHAYN,
GERMAN GENERAL

The only time he ever put up a fight was when we asked him to resign.
—GEORGES CLEMENCEAU, FRENCH PRIME
MINISTER, ON JOSEPH JOFFRE,
FRENCH GENERAL

Brilliant to the top of his army boots.

> —DAVID LLOYD GEORGE, BRITISH PRIME
> MINISTER, ON FIELD MARSHAL DOUGLAS
> HAIG

A dour Scotsman and the dullest dog I ever had the happiness to meet.

> —SIR PHILIP WALHOUSE, LORD CHETWODE,
> ON FIELD MARSHAL DOUGLAS HAIG

What a rascal Haig was. One of the biggest rascals in a long time. . . . Oh, he is a disgraceful story.

Haig was devoid of the gift of intelligible and coherent expression.

> —LORD BEAVERBROOK, ON FIELD MARSHAL
> DOUGLAS HAIG

If Kitchener was not a great man, he was at least, a great poster.

—Margot Asquith, wife of Prime Minister Herbert Asquith, on Lord Kitchener, British general whose visage graced Britain's World War I recruiting posters

He stands aloof and alone, a molten mass of devouring energy and burning ambition, without anybody to control or guide it in the right direction.

—Lord Curzon, Conservative politician, on Lord Kitchener

Kitchener is not attractive. None of the men who served with him were attracted to him. It is the coarseness of his fibre, which appears in his face to a marked degree. The eyes are good—but the jaw and skin are those of a rough private.

—Lord Esher, deputy governor of Windsor Castle, on Lord Kitchener

THEIR FINEST HOUR

Nothing makes for more fertile ground for insult than outsize personalities, and World War II supplied a host of them. Patton, Monty, MacArthur, Ike—each was as temperamental as he was brilliant, and each one vied for credit for Allied successes with political leaders and fellow generals. Conditions were ripe for a major slagfest. . . .

ON DOUGLAS MACARTHUR

MacArthur is the type of man who thinks that when he gets to heaven, God will step down from the great white throne and bow him into His vacated seat.

　　—HAROLD L. ICKES, U.S. PRESIDENTIAL AIDE

I didn't fire him because he was a dumb son of a bitch, although he was, but that's not against the law for generals.

　　—HARRY S TRUMAN

Never trust a man who combs his hair straight from his left armpit.

　　—ALICE ROOSEVELT LONGWORTH, DAUGHTER
　　　OF THEODORE ROOSEVELT

I studied dramatics under him for twelve years.
—DWIGHT D. EISENHOWER

ON BERNARD MONTGOMERY

In defeat unbeatable, in victory unbearable.
—WINSTON CHURCHILL

He's just a little man, he's just as little inside as he is outside.

He got so damn personal to make sure that the Americans and me, in particular, had no credit, had nothing to do with the war, that I eventually just stopped communicating with him. . . . I was just not interested in keeping up communications with a man that just can't tell the truth.

—DWIGHT D. EISENHOWER

Monty is a tired little fart. War requires the taking of risks and he won't take them.

 —GEORGE S. PATTON

ON DWIGHT D. EISENHOWER

The best clerk I ever fired.

 —DOUGLAS MACARTHUR

Ike didn't follow my advice. He lost a lot of lives. Eighty thousand American boys in the Ardennes alone. Damned fool Ike.

 —BERNARD MONTGOMERY

Every time I get a new star, I get attacked.
And every time you get attacked, I pull you out.

 —EXCHANGE BETWEEN GEN. DWIGHT D.
  EISENHOWER AND GEN. GEORGE S. PATTON

ON GEORGE S. PATTON

Patton's mouth does not always carry out the functions of his brain.

 —GEN. WALTER BEDELL SMITH

PATTON FIRES BACK

Gen. Patton was famous for never holding back—on the battlefield or when it came time to give his opinion. He often reserved his most pungent barbs for his own allies—many of whom were his rivals for space in the history books. Herewith Patton on . . .

GEN. OMAR BRADLEY

A man of great mediocrity.

Bradley is a good officer, but he utterly lacks 'it.' Too bad.

GEN. BRADLEY AND GEN. COURTNEY HODGES

Bradley and Hodges are such nothings. Their virtue is that they get along by doing nothing.

Courtney Hodges and Omar Bradley both received a Distinguished Service Medal for their unsuccessful defense of the 'Bulge.' I did not receive one for successfully defending it.

GEN. MARK CLARK

It makes my flesh creep to be with him.

He seems to me more preoccupied with bettering his own future than in winning the war.

GEN. MARK CLARK AND GEN. DWIGHT EISENHOWER

They have no knowledge of men or war. Too damned slick, especially Clark.

EISENHOWER

Ike has no conception of physical command. He has never exercised it.

His is the style of an office seeker rather than that of a soldier.

Ike is bound hand and foot by the British and does not know it. Poor fool.

Ike was fine, except that he spoke of lunch as "tiffin," of gasoline as "petrol," and of antiaircraft as "flack." I truly fear that London has conquered Abilene.

Ike is not as rugged mentally as I had thought. He vacillates and is not realistic.

Chapter Four

GOD, I HATE THE ~~ENGLISH~~ ~~FRENCH RUSSIANS~~ AMERICANS

Imagine how different history would be without fervent nationalism, ethnic grudges, and cultural chauvinism. Would the Archduke Franz Ferdinand have taken the bullet that ignited World War I? Would the Germans and Poles have worked out their differences over small tracts of disputed land and averted World War II? How many historical events have been set into motion by national enmity built up over the centuries? This country-by-country rundown celebrates the important place irrational hatred of foreigners has played in forging our common destiny. Loathing, it seems, knows no border. . . .

AUSTRIA

A Bavarian is halfway between an Austrian and a human being.
—OTTO VON BISMARCK

The Austrian government . . . is a system of despotism tempered by casualness.
—VICTOR ADLER, CZECH-BORN SOCIAL DEMOCRATIC POLITICIAN

BELGIUM

Belgium is just a country invented by the British to annoy the French.
—CHARLES DE GAULLE

CANADA

Canada is useful only to provide me with furs.
—MADAME DE POMPADOUR, MISTRESS OF KING LOUIS XV

What a country! Here all the knaves grow rich and the honest men are ruined.

—Louis Joseph, Marquis de Montcalm

Toronto as a city carries out the idea of Canada as a country. It is a calculated crime both against the aspirations of the soul and the affection of the heart.

—Aleister Crowley, British magician and author

Quebec does not have opinions—only sentiments.

—Sir Wilfrid Laurier, Canadian prime minister

A rascally heap of sand, rock, and swamp, called Prince Edward Island, in the horrible Gulf of St. Lawrence; that lump of worthlessness . . . bears nothing but potatoes.

—William Cobbett, British radical journalist

British Columbia is a barren, cold, mountain country that is not worth keeping. . . . Fifty railroads would not galvanize it into prosperity.

—Henry Labouchere, British politician

DENMARK

There are three fine old kingdoms, over which the King of Denmark is Lord, although their subjects are all rough and uncouth.

—MAXIMILIAN I, HOLY ROMAN EMPEROR

EGYPT

I never saw a place I liked worse, nor which afforded less pleasure or instruction, nor antiquities which less answered their description.

—JAMES BRUCE, SCOTTISH EXPLORER

FRANCE

Have the Frenchman for thy friend; not for thy neighbor.

—NICEPHORUS I, BYZANTINE EMPEROR

The ignorance of French society gives one a rough sense of the infinite.

—JOSEPH E. RENAN, FRENCH PHILOLOGIST

You must hate a Frenchman as you hate the devil.
—Horatio Nelson, British naval
   commander

I do not dislike the French from the vulgar antipathy
between neighboring nations, but for their insolent
and unfounded airs of superiority.
—Horace Walpole, British writer and
   antiquarian

A despotism tempered by epigrams.
—Thomas Carlyle, British historian and
   essayist

How can one conceive of a one-party system in a
country that has over two hundred varieties of
cheeses?
—Charles de Gaulle

A small acquaintance with history shows that all
governments are selfish and the French governments
more selfish than most.
—Viscount Eccles, British politician and
   patron of the arts

The Almighty in His infinite wisdom did not see fit
to create Frenchmen in the image of Englishmen.
　—Winston Churchill

GERMANY

Germans have no taste for peace. . . . When not
engaged in warfare, they spend some little time in
hunting, but more in idling, abandoned to sleep and
gluttony.
　—Tacitus, Roman historian

I wish I were a stork and the Germans were frogs in
the marshes, so I could devour them all; or else a
pike in a lake and they fish, so I could eat them this
way.
　—Pope Martin IV

The godless Germans.
　—Ivan the Terrible

I speak Spanish to God, Italian to women, French to
men, and German to my horse.
　—Charles V, Holy Roman Emperor

The history of Germany is a history of . . . the licentiousness of the strong, and the oppression of the weak . . . , of general imbecility, confusion, and misery.
—ALEXANDER HAMILTON

A German singer! I should as soon expect to get pleasure from the neighing of my horse.
—FREDERICK THE GREAT

War is Prussia's national industry.
—COUNT MIRABEAU, FRENCH STATESMAN

Prussia is a country without any bottom, and in my opinion could not maintain a war for six weeks.
—BENJAMIN DISRAELI

Germany has reduced savagery to a science, and this great war for the victorious peace of justice must go on until the German cancer is cut clean out of the world body.
—THEODORE ROOSEVELT

For many years her professors, philosophers, and so-called thinkers inculcated the theory that she was superior to all other countries and, therefore, had the

right to do with them whatever she would. The rules of morality, apparently, did not apply to Germany.
　　—FERDINAND FOCH, FRENCH GENERAL

Thirty centuries of history enable us to look with majestic pity at certain doctrines taught on the other side of the Alps by the descendants of people who were wholly illiterate in the days when Rome boasted a Caesar, a Virgil, and an Augustus.

I should be pleased, I suppose, that Hitler has carried out a revolution on our lines. But they are Germans. So they will end by ruining our idea.

　　—BENITO MUSSOLINI

The Hun is always either at your throat or at your feet.
　　—WINSTON CHURCHILL

You must look out in England that you are not
cheated by the charioteers.
—MARCUS TULLIUS CICERO

The perfidious, haughty, savage, disdainful, stupid,
slothful, inhospitable, inhuman English.
—JULIUS CAESAR SCALIGER, ITALIAN
PHILOLOGIST

The English are, in my opinion, perfidious and
cunning, plotting the destruction of the lives of
foreigners, so that even if they humbly bend the
knee, they cannot be trusted.
—LEO OF ROZMITAL, BROTHER OF THE KING OF
BOHEMIA

England, the heart of a rabbit in the body of a lion,
the jaws of a serpent in an abode of popinjays.
—EUSTACHE DESCHAMPS, FRENCH BALLADEER
AND SATIRIST

The English take their pleasures sadly, after the fashion of their country.

—MAXIMILIEN DE BÉTHUNE, FRENCH STATESMAN

A pirate spreading misery and ruin over the face of the ocean.

—THOMAS JEFFERSON

The English are not an inventive people; they don't eat enough pie.

—THOMAS EDISON

NO WONDER HE HATED WELLINGTON

England is a nation of shopkeepers.

The English have no exalted sentiments. They can all be bought.

The English often kill themselves—it is a malady caused by the humid climate.

—NAPOLEON BONAPARTE

The mere scum of the earth.
—THE DUKE OF WELLINGTON, ON THE
BRITISH SOLDIER

Unmitigated noodles.
—KAISER WILHELM II, ON THE ENGLISH
PEOPLE

It is my royal and imperial command that you . . .
exterminate first the treacherous English, and . . .
walk over General French's contemptible little army.
—KAISER WILHELM II, REFERRING TO THE
BRITISH EXPEDITIONARY FORCE

It is noticeable that most of the American officers
here are pro British, even Ike. I am not, repeat not,
pro British.
—GEORGE S. PATTON

The English never draw a line without blurring it.
—WINSTON CHURCHILL

> Paralytic sycophants, effete betrayers of humanity,
> carrion-eating servile imitators, arch-cowards and
> collaborators, gang of women-murderers, degenerate
> rabble, parasitic traditionalists, playboy soldiers,
> conceited dandies.
> —EAST GERMAN COMMUNIST PARTY'S
> APPROVED TERMS OF ABUSE FOR EAST
> GERMAN SPEAKERS WHEN DESCRIBING
> BRITAIN, 1953

INDIA

India is a geographical term. It is no more a united
nation than the Equator.
—WINSTON CHURCHILL

I suppose the real difficulty is an utter lack of courage,
moral and political, amongst the natives.
—GEORGE V, KING OF ENGLAND

IRELAND

The Irish militia are useless in times of war and
dangerous in times of peace.
—THE DUKE OF WELLINGTON

The bane of England, and the opprobrium of Europe.
  —Benjamin Disraeli

You've got to exchange the populations of Holland
and Ireland. Then the Dutch will turn Ireland into a
beautiful garden and the Irish will forget to mend the
dikes and will all be drowned.
  —Otto von Bismarck

What a bloody awful country.
  —Reginald Maudling, British
    Conservative politician

ITALY

All Italians are plunderers.
  —Napoleon Bonaparte

The whipped jackal . . . frisking by the side of the
German tiger.
  —Winston Churchill

It is not maligning the Italians to describe their
achievements, from the purely military standpoint, as
extraordinarily small.
  —Erich von Falkenhayn, German general

JAPAN

> It becomes still more difficult to reconcile Japanese action with prudence or even with sanity.
> —WINSTON CHURCHILL

Little yellow men who sit up all night thinking how to screw us.
—EDITH CRESSON, FRENCH PRIME MINISTER

The Japanese are a disease of the skin. The Communists are a disease of the heart.
—CHIANG KAI-SHEK, CHINESE NATIONALIST LEADER

I stand by the opinion that the Japs are bastards.
—ADMIRAL WILLIAM F. "BULL" HALSEY, U.S. NAVAL COMMANDER

THE NETHERLANDS

Compared with Greece and Italy, Holland is but a platter-faced, cold-gin-and-water country, after all, and a heavy, barge-built, web-footed race are its inhabitants.

 —SIR FRANCIS BOND HEAD, BRITISH
   ADMINISTRATOR

Amsterdam, Rotterdam, and all the other dams!
Damned if I'll go.

 —KING GEORGE V

What a po-faced lot these Dutch are!

 —PRINCE PHILIP, HUSBAND OF QUEEN
   ELIZABETH II

POLAND

Our eternal foes, the Poles.

 —NICHOLAS I, CZAR OF RUSSIA

That bastard of the Versailles Treaty.

 —VYACHESLAV MOLOTOV, SOVIET FOREIGN
   MINISTER

There are few virtues which the Poles do not possess
and there are few errors they have ever avoided.

 —WINSTON CHURCHILL

RUSSIA

Scratch the Russian and you will find the Tartar.
—JOSEPH DE MAISTRE, FRENCH DIPLOMAT

Absolutism tempered by assassination.
—COUNT MÜNSTER, HANOVERIAN DIPLOMAT

Oh, if the Queen were a man, she would like to go and give those Russians, whose word one cannot believe, such a beating!
—QUEEN VICTORIA

Their people are unwarlike, their officials corrupt, their rulers only competent when borrowed from Germany.
—MARQUIS OF SALISBURY, BRITISH STATESMAN

The future belongs to Russia, which grows and grows, looming above us as an increasingly terrifying nightmare.
—THEOBALD VON BETHMANN HOLLWEG, GERMAN CHANCELLOR

From being a patriotic myth, the Russian people have become an awful reality.

—LEON TROTSKY

In Russia a man is called reactionary if he objects to having his property stolen and his wife and children murdered.

—WINSTON CHURCHILL

Russian communism is the illegitimate child of Karl Marx and Catherine the Great.

—CLEMENT ATTLEE, BRITISH PRIME MINISTER

SCOTLAND

A country so much our enemy that there is hardly any intelligence to be got, and whenever we do procure any it is the business of the country to have it contradicted.

—THE DUKE OF CUMBERLAND,
   BRITISH GENERAL

SERBIA

To have to go to war on account of tiresome Serbia beggars belief.
—QUEEN MARY, WIFE OF KING GEORGE V

SPAIN

All evil comes from Spain; all good from the north.
—SIR THOMAS CHALONER, BRITISH WRITER
AND SOLDIER

A whale stranded upon the seashore of Europe.
—EDMUND BURKE

SWITZERLAND

A country to be in for two hours, to two and a half if the weather is fine, and no more. Ennui comes in the third hour, and suicide attacks you before the night.
—LORD BROUGHAM, BRITISH
PARLIAMENTARIAN

I look upon Switzerland as an inferior sort of
Scotland.

—Sydney Smith, British essayist

TURKEY

Let me endeavor, very briefly to sketch, in the rudest
outline what the Turkish race was and what it is. . . .
They were, upon the whole, from the black day when
they first entered Europe, the one great antihuman
specimen of humanity. Wherever they went a broad
line of blood marked the track behind them, and, as
far as their dominion reached, civilization
disappeared from view.

—William Gladstone, British prime
minister

The barbarian power, which has been for centuries
seated in the very heart of the Old World, which has
in its brute clutch the most famous countries of
classical and religious antiquity and many of the most
fruitful and beautiful regions of the earth; and,

which, having no history itself, is heir to the historical names of Constantinople and Nicaea, Nicomedia and Caesarea, Jerusalem and Damascus, Nineva and Babylon, Mecca and Bagdad, Antioch and Alexandria, ignorantly holding in its possession one half of the history of the whole world.

—CARDINAL JOHN HENRY NEWMAN,
BRITISH DIVINE

Before World War I, Turkey was known as the sick man of Europe. Now it is almost terminal.

—RICHARD M. NIXON

UNITED STATES

Their disappearance from the human family would be no great loss to the world.

—HENRY CLAY, U.S. SENATOR, ON NATIVE
AMERICANS

Knavery seems to be so much the striking feature of its inhabitants that it may not in the end be an evil that they will become aliens to this country.

—GEORGE III, BRITISH MONARCH

God protects fools, drunks, and the United States of America.

—OTTO VON BISMARCK

I found there a country with thirty-two religions and only one sauce.

—CHARLES-MAURICE DE TALLEYRAND-PÉRIGORD, FRENCH DIPLOMAT AND STATESMAN

If I owned Texas and Hell, I would rent out Texas and live in Hell.

—GEN. PHILLIP H. SHERIDAN

America is the only nation in history which miraculously has gone directly from barbarism to degeneration without the usual interval of civilization.

—GEORGES CLEMENCEAU, FRENCH PRIME MINISTER

Americans always try to do the right thing—after they've tried everything else.

—WINSTON CHURCHILL

The Americans cannot build airplanes. They are very good at refrigerators and razor blades.

—HERMAN GOERING

The thing that impresses me most about America is the way parents obey their children.

—THE DUKE OF WINDSOR

America is the ultimate denial of the theory of man's continuous evolution.

—H. RAP BROWN, U.S. RADICAL

SLAMAGUNDI

Some insults defy categorization. Nevertheless, they're too good to be left out. To close the book on historical calumny, here's an international salad of some of history's choicest put-downs. . . .

The difference between us is that my family begins with me, whereas yours ends with you.

—IPHICRATES, ATHENIAN GENERAL, REPLYING TO A DESCENDANT OF HARMODIUS (AN ATHENIAN HERO), WHO HAD DERIDED HIM FOR BEING THE SON OF A COBBLER

Unfaithful bitch! Messalina! Medusa! Gorgon!
—ROMAN EMPEROR CLAUDIUS, TO HIS WIFE
MESSALINA

The more I read him, the less I wonder that they
poisoned him.
—THOMAS BABINGTON MACAULAY, BRITISH
WHIG POLITICIAN, ON SOCRATES

His mind was such that he could never believe
anything was done well unless he did it himself.
—SIR ROBERT MUNRO, SCOTTISH SOLDIER, ON
GUSTAVUS ADOLPHUS, KING OF SWEDEN

In eighteen months he won one battle, lost a second,
and was killed in the third. His fame was won at a
bargain price.
—NAPOLEON BONAPARTE, ON GUSTAVUS
ADOLPHUS, KING OF SWEDEN

A dangerous man, subtle, politic, professing to stand
by the people, to champion their interests . . . but
seeking only the favor of the mob, giving himself out

sometimes to stand as a Catholic, sometimes as a Calvinist or Lutheran.

> —Cardinal Nicholas Granvelle, on
> William of Orange, Dutch statesman

The other fool who wasted his time fighting the Turks.

> —Nicholas I, czar of Russia, on John III,
> king of Poland

I heard him once, and it was as low, confused, puerile, conceited, ill-natured, enthusiastic a performance as I ever heard.

> —Jonathan Mayhew, Calvinist
> churchman, on George Whitefield,
> Calvinist churchman

He is a silk stocking filled with dung.

> —Napoleon Bonaparte, on Charles-
> Maurice de Talleyrand-Périgord,
> French statesman

His mind was a kind of extinct sulphur-pit.

> —Thomas Carlyle, British historian and
> essayist, on Napoelon III

Strip your Louis Quatorze of his king-gear, and there is left nothing but a poor forked radish with a head fantastically carved—admirable to no valet.

—THOMAS CARLYLE, BRITISH HISTORIAN AND ESSAYIST, ON LOUIS XIV, KING OF FRANCE

A tart Luther who neighs like a horse.

—RALPH WALDO EMERSON, U.S. AUTHOR, ON WILLIAM LLOYD GARRISON, U.S. ABOLITIONIST

The arch-Philistine Jeremy Bentham was the insipid, pedantic, leather-tongued oracle of the bourgeois intelligence of the nineteenth century.

—KARL MARX, ON JEREMY BENTHAM, BRITISH POLITICAL PHILOSOPHER

Boastful, egotistic, tyrannical, intolerant, cunning, shifty, smooth and suave, avaricious . . . A sheer opportunist and a demagogic charlatan.

—ROBERT W. BAGNALL, NAACP OFFICIAL, ON MARCUS GARVEY, BLACK NATIONALIST LEADER

You show the bourgeoisie your behind. We, on the contrary, look them in the face.

—Georgi Valentinovich Plekhanov, Russian social democrat, to Vladimir Ilyich Lenin

It was the supreme expression of the mediocrity of the apparatus that Stalin himself rose to his position.

—Leon Trotsky, on Josef Stalin

How many divisions has he got?

—Josef Stalin, on Pope Pius XI

Like Peter the Great, Stalin fought barbarism with barbarism.

—Nikita Khruschev, on Josef Stalin

CHURCHILLIAN WIT

Winston Churchill is rightly considered one of the masters of English prose. Never was his way with words more in evidence than when he was insulting his fellow world leaders. Herewith Churchill on . . .

ADOLF HITLER

A bloodthirsty guttersnipe, a monster of wickedness, insatiable in his lust for blood and plunder.

This wicked man, the repository and embodiment of soul-destroying hatred, the monstrous product of former wrongs and shames.

If Hitler were to invade Hell, I would find occasion to make a favorable reference to the devil.

BENITO MUSSOLINI

Italy's pinchbeck Ceasar.

CHARLES DE GAULLE

What can you do with a man who looks like a female llama surprised when bathing?

Just look at him! He might be Stalin with two hundred divisions.

MOHANDAS K. GANDHI

A seditious Middle Temple lawyer, now posing as a fakir of a type well known in the East.

MOSHE DAYAN

Don't be so humble, you're not that great.

> —GOLDA MEIR, ISRAELI PRIME MINISTER, TO
> MOSHE DAYAN, ISRAELI DEFENSE MINISTER